# Dining at Delmonico's

STEWART, TABORI & CHANG
New York

# Dining at Delmonico's

## The Story of America's Oldest Restaurant

JUDITH CHOATE *and* JAMES CANORA

PHOTOGRAPHS BY STEVE POOL

Published in 2008 by Stewart, Tabori & Chang
An imprint of Harry N. Abrams, Inc.

HISTORICAL PHOTOGRAPHS
page 10: © Photo Collection Alexander Alland, Sr.; page 11: Museum of the City of New York; pages 14 and 15: Collection of the New-York Historical Society; pages 17 (top right and center), 21 (top and bottom), 22, 23, 27: Museum of the City of New York/Byron Collection; page 17 (bottom and bottom left): © Bettmann/Corbis; pages 19 (bottom left) and 29 (top, center, and bottom): Rare Books Division, The New York Public Library, Astor, Lenox and Tilden Foundation; page 69: Hutton Archives/Getty Images

Library of Congress Cataloging-in-Publication Data

Choate, Judith.
Dining at Delmonico's : a trip through time at New York's oldest restaurant
by Judith Choate and James Canora.
p. cm.
ISBN 978-1-58479-722-7
1. Delmonico's Restaurant (New York, N.Y.)—History. 2. Cookery. I. Canora, James. II. Title.

TX945.5.D4C56 2008
641.59747—dc22
2008007815

Editor: Luisa Weiss
Designed by Joel Avirom, Jason Snyder, and Meghan Day Healey
Production Manager: Tina Cameron

The text of this book was composed in Garamond.

Printed and bound in China
10 9 8 7 6 5 4 3 2 1

**HNA**
**harry n. abrams, inc.**
a subsidiary of La Martinière Groupe
115 West 18th Street
New York, NY 10011
www.hnabooks.com

# Acknowledgments

*From Milan Licul:*

I am deeply grateful for the love of my late parents. Their advice, leadership, and courage gave me the inspiration and fortitude to succeed in my adopted country.

It is with the deepest gratitude that I thank my longtime partner and dearest friend, Branko Turcinovic, for his faith and support in all of our ventures and particularly for his enthusiastic endorsement of Delmonico's.

My gratitude also to my partners Omer and Fred Grgurev, who are always there to offer guidance and support.

And to the staff at Delmonico's led by Dennis Turcinovic, managing partner, and Corrado Goglia, general manager, I extend my deepest thanks for your devotion to the restaurant and to our goals. Delmonico's has grown and prospered because of your faithfulness.

To our customers, you are all deeply appreciated.

*From Judith Choate and James Canora:*

Blessings to Milan Licul and the entire staff of Delmonico's for making this book possible.

To Mama Faye and Papa Vito Canora for love, support, and laughs. And to Mama for letting us borrow her beautiful Italian tableware and linen for this book.

To Angelina Duffy and Rosemarie Caruso for their generous gift of so many marvelous pieces of tableware and silver for our photography sessions.

To Steve Mohr of More and More Antiques, we couldn't have done it without your knowledge and generosity.

To Rick Dodge of Rick Dodge Antiques, your knowledge and kindness made us look very good.

To Joel Avirom, Meghan Day Healey, and Jason Snyder, your hand-holding throughout and your shared gift of history made our job very much easier.

Special thanks to Dragan Mavra and Valter Morovic of Time Café, who very generously lent us their kitchen and staff.

To Poppa—Mr. Woody—or as others know him, Steve Pool, we say "Scungill" for making everything we cooked look spectacular.

Special thanks to Jay Rosengarten, Samia Murtaza, Joey and John Dier, Aris Mixon, Lynn Marsh, and Doug DeLong.

*From James Canora:*

With much appreciation and love to my entire family, Mom and Dad, Peter and Joanne, Samantha and Louis, Marie and Moe, Adam, Zachary, and Sammy, and all of my aunts, uncles, and cousins who make up one great big wonderful family.

Much gratitude to Don Pintabona for ten years of mentoring and many more of friendship.

Thanks also to Jane Rosenthal for always believing in me and for your guidance and support.

And thanks to my buddy, Michael Stewart of Tavern on Jane, who is always there with a kitchen and a pop!

James Stewart, for your impeccable special event and organizational skills (Intermedia Production Group).

Rosalie and Shelly Friedland, for your longtime support, knowledge, and advice.

Lt. Jay Fagan, for your warmth and charm and years of keeping us safe, sound, and secure.

Continental Airlines Food Service Division, Sandra, Sigi, Gerry, Robin, Sashi, Victor, Cynthia, Tammy Briggs, and the rest of the fine staff at Chelsea Kitchens in Houston and Newark.

# Contents

# Preface

You might say that I was in the restaurant business even before I was born. My mother worked in the small café and general store that my parents owned until two hours before I arrived. However, growing up in Croatia I had no idea that I would one day own one of the most highly regarded restaurants in the world, a restaurant whose long-departed founders remain, 170 years later, honored citizens in their native Switzerland. It has been, for me, the realization of a dream.

When my family immigrated to America, the restaurant business offered a chance to earn extra money while I improved my language skills. And, believe me, the money that I earned seemed a fortune after years of struggling in a Communist-run country. Although I eventually trained to be an electrical engineer, at the time I received my degree there were very few entry-level jobs, and I retreated back to restaurant work.

As I matured, I found that I truly loved the business. I loved the routine of running the front of the house, the mechanics of keeping the kitchen humming, and most of all I enjoyed meeting the many different people I served. Thriftiness was in my nature, and in a short time I was able to save enough money to form a partnership to open a small Italian restaurant. From this tiny beginning, we have been fortunate to be able to expand our enterprise to include a number of restaurants throughout New York City.

The jewel in our crown is Delmonico's. Its old-world atmosphere and opulent setting is, to me, the culmination of any restaurateur's aspirations. I like to reflect on the hopes and dreams of the Delmonico brothers as they took luxury to its limits in the expansion of their restaurant empire, knowing that we are taking the classic American steakhouse to its ideal. It is my hope that I will have the opportunity to welcome each of you to my restaurant home, the original Delmonico's at South William and Beaver Streets in New York City. Your table is waiting,

*Milan Licul*
*Managing Partner, Ocinomled Group*

Milan Licul

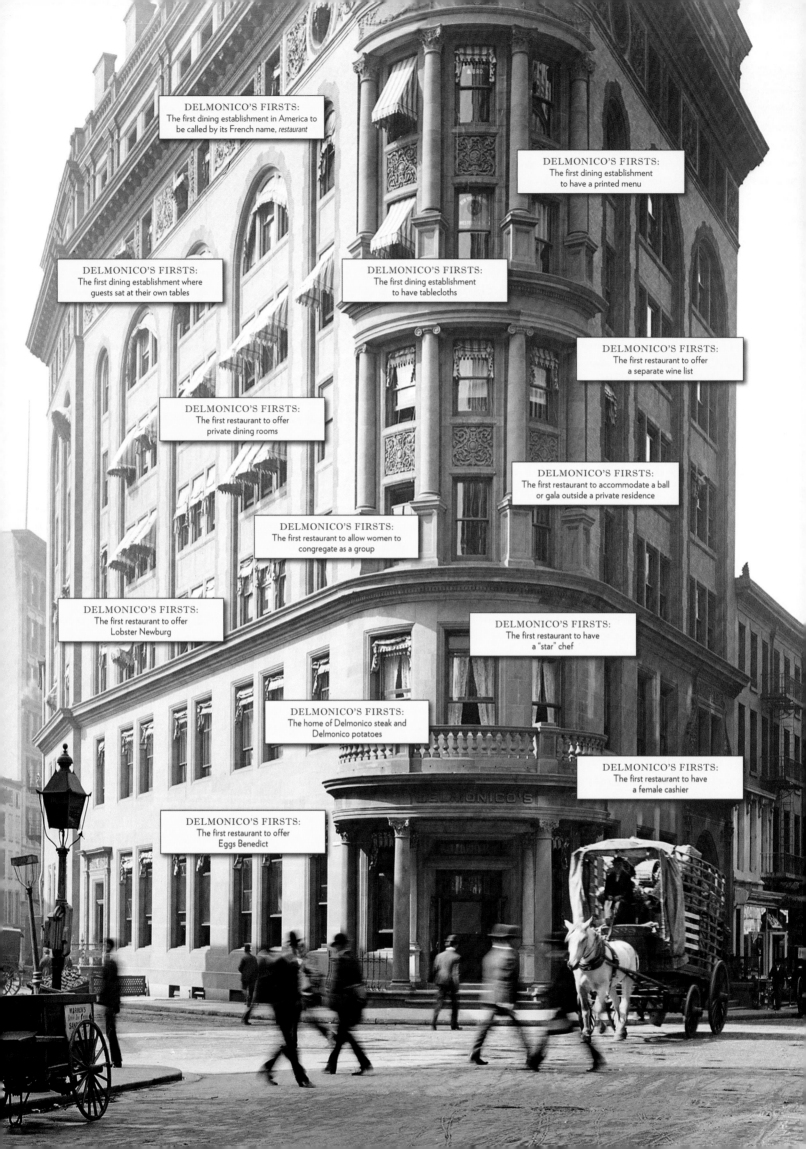

**DELMONICO'S FIRSTS:**
The first dining establishment in America to be called by its French name, *restaurant*

**DELMONICO'S FIRSTS:**
The first dining establishment to have a printed menu

**DELMONICO'S FIRSTS:**
The first dining establishment where guests sat at their own tables

**DELMONICO'S FIRSTS:**
The first dining establishment to have tablecloths

**DELMONICO'S FIRSTS:**
The first restaurant to offer a separate wine list

**DELMONICO'S FIRSTS:**
The first restaurant to offer private dining rooms

**DELMONICO'S FIRSTS:**
The first restaurant to accommodate a ball or gala outside a private residence

**DELMONICO'S FIRSTS:**
The first restaurant to allow women to congregate as a group

**DELMONICO'S FIRSTS:**
The first restaurant to offer Lobster Newburg

**DELMONICO'S FIRSTS:**
The first restaurant to have a "star" chef

**DELMONICO'S FIRSTS:**
The home of Delmonico steak and Delmonico potatoes

**DELMONICO'S FIRSTS:**
The first restaurant to have a female cashier

**DELMONICO'S FIRSTS:**
The first restaurant to offer Eggs Benedict

# A Historical Perspective

**B**ecause its legend is woven into both the history of New York City and the evolution of fine dining in America, the story of Delmonico's Restaurant reads like a fairy tale. Lush with adventuring, myth, extravagance, prevarication, romance, morality fables, and profligacy, it is a saga that follows the explosion of wealth in America while it remains the ultimate American success story. So, we begin the tale.

Once upon a time—in actual fact the year was 1824—a successful Swiss schooner captain, Giovanni Del-Monico, left his sea legs behind for a life on solid ground in America. Why, we do not know, but his knowledge of the products traded between the United States, Spain, and Cuba, most specifically the barrels of wine and spirits, led him to open a modest wine shop near New York City's Battery. Purchasing everyday wine inexpensively barreled, Captain Del-Monico bottled and sold it at a sizable profit to the business community that was beginning to develop in lower Manhattan.

After two years working to build a thriving business, the Captain, who had by this time adopted New York as his home and anglicized his name to John Del-Monico, closed his small shop and returned to Switzerland. Rather than signaling the end of his career, it was a signal of his faith in its future. His astute business sense led him to seek family counsel and assistance before embarking on expansion in the rapidly growing metropolis he now called home. He felt that as the city developed and a new class of entrepreneurs matured, there would be a growing demand for the luxuries that riches would value, luxuries that he could provide with the help of his brother, Pietro Antonio, a successful confectioner in Berne.

Winning his brother's interest, John, with Peter (as Pietro would now be known), sailed for New York, where they pooled their not-inconsequential resources of $20,000. John's skill in the wine trade and Peter's mastery of the pastry arts led them to establish a European-style pastry shop and café in the heart of the burgeoning business district. It was unlike any other spot in the city, at 23 William Street, a rented location that was within walking distance of the entire district.

Although business was conducted as Del-Monico and Brother, John and Peter worked as equals as they built their house of hospitality and fine food. Their enterprise was an instant success, attracting European residents and business travelers to the warmth of a familiar social setting as well as American businessmen seeking a comfortable spot to conduct informal

OPPOSITE: Delmonico's, a treasure trove of American firsts, as the front appeared in 1889

BELOW: Delmonico's first menu, 1838

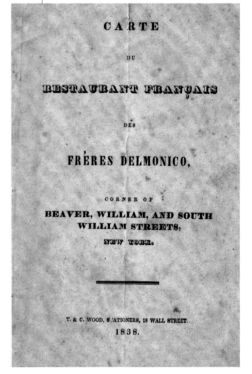

Classic French pastries as served at the original Delmonico's pastry shop

meetings and a respite from daily activities. For many years it was assumed that a sign painter had mistakenly spelled the family name as Delmonico on the café's sign. However, most historians believe that the brothers were such sticklers for perfection that they would never have allowed such a mistake to persist. It is now believed that it was the brothers' wish to adopt a more American-sounding version of their family name that led to the change. Whatever occurred, the spelling remained.

The café was homespun in look and feel. Simple pine tables and chairs were the sole customer seating, and the tableware consisted of simple spoons, two-tined forks with bone handles, and rustic earthenware plates and mugs. Each day the cakes and pastries were displayed on a pine counter covered in fresh white napkins, and it is said that Peter, dressed in his chef's apron and hat, served them with a flourish. John ran the business and dispensed good cheer along with coffee, chocolate, wines, liquors, bonbons, and cigars. The cakes cost a penny; coffee, hot chocolate, or cognacs were supplied at six cents a drink; and the best Havana cigar was sold for the same few pennies. To keep it all in the family, Peter's wife was the friendly cashier, an unheard-of job for a woman in America.

Almost from the moment it opened, the shop was extremely successful. It offered a pleasant break for businessmen and travelers, who could simply enjoy a warm drink or libation, smoke a stogie, or have a light snack and some good conversation. The pastries and other goodies were of superior quality, the coffee and other drinks the best to be had, and the hosts hospitable and caring. Heretofore, meals were taken at home, carried in a pocket, box, or basket, or eaten in an inn or hotel dining room. The new concept of a light snack taken in the mellow atmosphere of a family-run café was quickly absorbed into the daily routine of commercial activity.

As the business prospered, the Delmonico brothers expanded into a room next door at 25 William Street and then followed that expansion by renting the entire building in 1830. They had quickly gone from Del-Monico & Brother, Confectioners, to Delmonico & Brother, Confectioners, and Restaurant

Français, the latter the genesis of the fine dining empire that was to come. This had required bringing additional family members from Switzerland, as well as the hiring of French chefs to execute the menus that the brothers conceived. The original pastry shop remained at 23 William while the restaurant, now considered the very first public dining room or restaurant in the United States, occupied number 25.

The restaurant was such a ground-breaking idea that it quickly became the talk of the town. Everyone had to try it! It featured a "carte," or menu, a new amenity at this point, with the dishes listed in both English *and* French (an even more original idea that would be imitated by others for years to come). The meals were prepared by a troupe of French cooks and starred French foods and dishes far outside the norm of American cooking. Patrons were allowed the privilege of selecting their own dishes, each separately priced, as was the Parisian custom. This was unlike the traditional American "ordinary," a set meal served at a set price in hotels and inns. The impeccable staff, trained by the Delmonicos, was polished and courtly. And the Delmonicos were the consummate hosts.

At this first Delmonico's establishment, diners tasted artichokes, eggplant, tomatoes, and endive, among other unfamiliar ingredients, for the first time. The new, lighter sauces devised by the famed French chef Antonin Câreme were introduced. An extensive wine list was initiated. Purveyors were courted and enticed into production and importation of the high-quality ingredients demanded by the owners. Quality was the deciding factor in everything that the brothers did. In fact, it was in this modest setting that the foundations of the modern premier restaurant business were set.

Of all the innovation and change that was to occur in this first restaurant setting, the most important was the inclusion, in 1831, of Lorenzo Delmonico. Lorenzo came to John and Peter as a young man of nineteen. The son of their brother, Francesco (who had remained in Switzerland), Lorenzo was sent to help his uncles as they expanded their business. It seemed as though he had been touched by a most hospitable star—he would be the guiding light of

Delmonico's for the next forty years. It was his leadership, business acumen, fine character, and discretion when dealing with clients that led Delmonico's to its international repute.

As extraordinary as it might seem, the Delmonico brothers were buying locally in the 1830s. In 1834, John and Peter had purchased a 220-acre farm in what was then known as Williamsburg, Long Island, an area that later was incorporated into the borough of Brooklyn. John built an imposing estate comprised of a main house, gardens, stables, and other outbuildings suitable to a grand home. Gardeners were employed to tend the plots and animals that could furnish the restaurant with the freshest produce, eggs, and meats possible.

With the café and restaurant thriving, the brothers added a lodging house at 76 Broad Street to their portfolio. It was, as was the norm in those days, a simple rooming house where most tenants were salesmen or foreign businessmen whose long-term appointments necessitated a permanent address without the requirements of a home. Set meals were served at a set time with none of the innovation seen at the restaurant. As simple as it was, this spot would serve as insurance for the Delmonicos' future.

In December 1835, an inferno swept lower Manhattan, destroying many buildings and businesses, including the William Street café and restaurant. Fortunately, the inn at 76 Broad Street was untouched, and it was there that the family showed its true colors. Led by the original brothers and Lorenzo, who had by now joined his uncles in the daily management of the businesses, a portion of the lodging house was quickly reconfigured as a restaurant, and within a couple of months, the Delmonicos were again serving their loyal clientele.

While working on reestablishing their credentials in the restaurant trade after the devastating fire, the brothers purchased land at the corner of Beaver, William, and South William streets. They intended to construct a restaurant that would reflect their determination to become America's transcendent restaurateurs. It was from this spot that their fame would spread across the world.

After extensive planning and attention to detail that was unique in the restaurant trade, Delmonico's Restaurant opened at 2 South William Street in

August 1837. The entire three-and-a-half-story building was devoted to fine service. The corner entrance featured marble pillars that had been excavated in Pompeii. The dining rooms on the two main floors displayed inlaid wood and marble floors, parquetry that was not seen even in the finest homes in the city. The walls were shiny with gilt, and the draperies were damasks of silk and satin. The third floor was all private dining rooms, a refinement not offered in any other establishment at that time. The finest china and silver glistened on the tabletops. The wine cellar caused much talk, as it was more than a hundred feet under street level and held 16,000 bottles of the finest wines the world had to offer. The kitchens were huge and staffed by a battery of skilled chefs, butchers, and pastry makers. For approximately $100,000, a very substantial amount at this time, the Delmonicos had built New York's first temple to haute cuisine. And in this lavish setting, they made it clear that they were "hosts," not just proprietors, a standard that is still sought by restaurateurs the world over.

As one can imagine, the restaurant set tongues wagging in small-town New York. However, it quickly became the "in" place to dine, and its adoring public called it "the Citadel," a name that clearly stated its import to polite society. It was here that Lorenzo Delmonico with his chef, John Lux, would create the luxurious meals that would translate to entertainment for the citizens of New York and the world. Businessmen, celebrities, politicians, and social wags all gathered to be seen in their care. Their skill was in such demand that the two even "catered" balls and dinners away from the restaurant, once transporting meals as far away as Newport, Rhode Island, to honor a visiting French dignitary. This at a time when a journey to the upper reaches of Manhattan took half a day over dirt passages!

As is often true in contemporary restaurants, the "scene" at Delmonico's was equal to the meals served. At this point in history, women did not dine in public, so one can only imagine the camaraderie of the gentlemen in attendance at meal times. Fine wines and after-dinner liqueurs flowed, rich, pungent cigars were ever-present, and gossip made the rounds of every table. Although the restaurant featured the most innovative recipes from the kitchens of Parisian chefs, the dishes were said to rise way above their origins in the New World setting as they blossomed with the abundance of superb American products.

With the death of John Delmonico in 1842, Lorenzo Delmonico became the titular head of all Delmonico enterprises. He was twenty-nine years old and not only had a full understanding of the refinements of playing host to New York's finest families, he also had supreme confidence in the future of New York as the financial center of the world and of his place in it. As Lorenzo stepped up to the demands of his life, he set an unchanging routine to ensure that all his obligations could be met in the day. He began each day in the wee hours of the morning, shopping the markets for the ingredients necessary for the day's menus. He would return to his office by eight or so, carrying with him the day's purchases. He would have his first cigar of the day and briefly go over any paperwork that required his attention. He would then stroll to his nearby home to rest for most of the day. By dinner time, he would return to the restaurant, where he would spend the evening supervising his staff and meeting and greeting his guests until his duties were done, around midnight. This routine is still followed by many restaurateurs today—generally without the cigars, however!

In 1845, another fire swept through lower Manhattan, this time taking with it the original lodging house at 76 Broad Street. While the restaurant did occupy much of Lorenzo's time, he felt that as the city expanded up and across town, so should Delmonico's. In 1846, Delmonico's Hotel at 25 Broadway (just above

OPPOSITE: The first Delmonico's at the corner of Beaver, William, and South William Streets

ABOVE: Lorenzo Delmonico

Bowling Green) replaced the simple lodging house as the Delmonicos' foray into the lodging business. It was the first hotel in the United States that was operated on the European plan whereby room and board were separate entities, with the meal "à la carte" (each item separately priced and purchased off a menu). Up to this point, all hotels and inns furnished both room and board for one inclusive price. For the most part, Delmonico's Hotel was solely Lorenzo's responsibility. His surviving uncle, Peter, had little interest in it—so little, in fact, that in 1849 he sold his interest in the family ventures to Lorenzo and retired.

From this point until his death in 1881, Lorenzo (by now known as Lorenzo the Great) was recognized as one of the world's leaders in the hospitality industry. The hotel thrived for the ten years that Lorenzo held the lease. Its rooms were the first choice of visiting celebrities, such as the celebrated Swedish songstress Jenny Lind and prominent United States military figure and presidential candidate General Winfield Scott. As American businessmen seemed to prefer a bar rather than the traditional French café, the hotel featured a bar where men could congregate for business and pleasure, enjoying fine wines and smoking their ever-present cigars.

In 1856, Lorenzo opened yet another restaurant on the corner of Broadway and Chambers Street, opposite City Hall, to meet the needs of his loyal clientele. All measure of businessmen, politicians, and lawyers met for lunch, while the dinner hours found the city's "best" at the tables, discriminating diners socializing, gossiping, and enjoying the cachet that was Delmonico's alone. The prices were high, the food superb, and the hospitality at its pinnacle.

This period was the beginning of the growth of Manhattan's financial prowess. It was during this time that American Express, among other long-lasting financial institutions, set the standards for America's future impact on the world of finance and business. It had made its headquarters on Hudson Street in 1854 and with prosperity moved to Broadway and Trinity Place by the 1870s, the defined area for financial success.

By the early 1860s Lorenzo had added another location farther uptown, on Union Square. Placed in a converted mansion on Fourteenth Street, this restaurant surpassed the expansive original to be called the "most luxurious restaurant in New York." It was managed by Lorenzo's nephew, Charles, who was then only twenty-two years old but had already proven his muster to his discerning uncle. This location featured both a restaurant and a café. The latter was considered the club of choice for both local and foreign notables with men of political, literary, business, and social consequence making a stop there part of their daily routine. It was also at this location that a major change in the dining room scene occurred, with the presence of women, to many a welcome addition. As you might note, as we track the progression of the Delmonico's businesses, we also track the evolution of cultural change and of Manhattan's business, political, and social communities up and across the city.

Perhaps the greatest culinary feat in American dining also occurred at the Fourteenth Street location when Lorenzo Delmonico hired Charles Ranhofer to

Through the years New York's elite dined in splendor at Delmonico's, except Harry K. Thaw, who required a personal delivery.

CLOCKWISE FROM TOP LEFT: On his second visit to America, Charles Dickens is pictured listening to an actor dressed as Mr. Pickwick discoursing over a splendid Delmonico's dinner; Mark Twain with guests in a Delmonico's private dining room, at his seventieth birthday celebration; Harry K. Thaw, wealthy man-about-town and accused murderer of the famed architect Stanford White, relishes a hand-delivered Delmonico's breakfast in the seclusion of his New York City jail cell; Impresario Billy Rose and his star, Gypsy Rose Lee, arriving at a party at Delmonico's celebrating fifty American firms founded in 1840; Delmonico's was the first restaurant to offer a meeting place for women, with the admittance of the Sorosis Society, an all-female club, in 1868.

be his *chef de cuisine*. Chef Ranhofer's skill in the kitchen more than matched Lorenzo's managerial abilities, and it was their combined efforts that ignited the worldwide fame of the restaurant. Ranhofer invented or reworked many famous dishes that remain synonomous with Delmonico's—Lobster Newburg (see page 178), Baked Alaska (see page 200), and Delmonico Steak (see page 126). He had a particular gift for naming dishes he invented after loyal customers or visiting celebrities, most notably at an 1868 dinner prepared in honor of Charles Dickens. Among the almost fifty items offered on the complete menu, diners found *Crème d'asperges à la Dumas*, *Pommes de terre Nelson*, *Côtelettes de grouse à la Fenimore Cooper*, and *Agneau farci à la Walter Scott*. Many of these recipes can be found in his epic tome, *The Epicurean*, an encyclopedia of American gastronomy that rivaled the revered *Mrs. Beeton's Book of Household Management* of English fame, which was first published in 1861. (Interestingly enough, Ranhofer had been preceded by Alessandro Filippini, who after leaving Delmonico's went on to become a well-known food consultant and compiler of cookery books. He also wrote a well-received cookbook called *The Table* in 1889. In this book, he noted that it was his intent to bring the Delmonico ideal to the home of the average American family of means.)

The 1868 Dickens dinner, sponsored by the New York Press Club, was important for a number of reasons. First and foremost, it caused Charles Dickens to apologize for his condemnation of the hospitality shown him by America in 1841–42. At that time, he had been honored by New York City's leading citizens at the cherished City Hotel with a banquet that was reported to be a model of gastronomy. However, Dickens clearly did not find his hosts up to his expectations and returned to England to satirize their boorishness in two books, *Martin Chuzzlewit* and *American Notes*. Under the leadership of the Delmonicos, hospitality in the New World had greatly changed during the forty years that had passed. On this subsequent trip Mr. Dickens found his hotel equal to those of Paris and his Delmonico meals (both private and at the banquet) to be unsurpassed anywhere in the world. In his speech he vowed to add an appendix to every republished copy of the two books stating that he had been received with "unsurpassable politeness, delicacy, sweet temper, hospitality, considerations . . ." by his American hosts.

When the New York Press Club announced the banquet, invitations were sent to members of the working press. As had been the norm through generations, no women were on the guest list. However, Jennie June Croly, the wife of the chairman of the inviting committee (David G. Croly, managing editor of the *New York World* newspaper), considered herself a member of the working press and applied for a ticket. Her application was met with amusement by her male counterparts and she was, of course, refused. She promptly notified other female members of the press, who applied for tickets and were not even acknowledged by the committee. Mrs. Croly, infuriated by this treatment, organized her coworkers into a press club of their own. (At this point in history there were absolutely no such clubs for women alone, and this defiance of cultural mores was looked upon with dismay.) They chose as their name the Sorosis Society, *sorosis* being an adaptation of a botanical word meaning an agglomeration, and went about the business of finding a convivial meeting place.

Horace Greeley, the influential editor and founder of the *New York Tribune*, when informed of the ladies' dismissal, told the inviting committee that he would not attend the Dickens banquet unless the women were treated with the respect due them. Unable to buck Mr. Greeley's influence, the committee found themselves in the position of having to ask the women to attend—if they did so as a group so just a few women would not be out of place. This further infuriated the women who, by this point, had decided that nothing could induce them to join the men. Since the male members of the New York Press Club had been meeting at Delmonico's for years, Mrs. Croly asked Lorenzo if her group could also use his restaurant as their gathering place. Lorenzo, as was his custom in welcoming all to dine, immediately put a private dining room at their disposal. So, on April 20, 1868, the first women-only organization held its first public meeting at Delmonico's, Fourteenth Street. It would continue to meet there for many years to come.

In 1865, yet another restaurant was necessary to accommodate the widening business clientele that demanded a table under the watchful eye of Lorenzo Delmonico, so he opened a rather unassuming spot at 22 Broad Street for the sole convenience of the new magnates in the stock market. It was not the usual over-the-top locale fancied by Lorenzo, but it immediately became the cherished hang-out for financial wizards and their followers. It is said that many of the schemes that floated the expansion of the United States economy were hatched at the tables of 22 Broad.

As Manhattan society moved north in the 1870s, Lorenzo decided to close the Fourteenth Street location and move its operation to Madison Square, the new center of town. This new restaurant, opened in 1876, occupied the entire south side of Twenty-sixth Street between Broadway and Fifth Avenue. It held a men's café; a main dining room covered in mirrors and swathed in silk, flowers, silver, and mahogany, with a fountain bubbling in the center of the room; a ballroom; a banquet hall; and a number of private dining rooms. There was even room for a few gentlemen residents on the

LEFT: The January 12, 1892, menu cover for a First Panel Sheriff's Jury dinner

ABOVE: A spoon commissioned from Tiffany & Co. by the New York City sheriff to be offered to members of a jury at a Delmonico's dinner. The handle holds the seal of the City of New York, resting on the word sheriff atop a fasces.

fourth floor and, on the fifth floor, enough space to quarter servants and store the necessities required for such an extravagant enterprise. It did not, however, have Chef Charles Ranhofer, who had retired to France, his homeland, upon the closing of the Fourteenth Street location.

The opening of the Madison Square spectacle was quickly followed by the closing of Chambers Street and the opening of another new place, at 112–114 Broadway near Pine Street, that was known as the Pine Street Restaurant. It was opened to attract the harried businessman with a quick-serve counter on the main floor, and it had the fine dining restaurant and private dining rooms upstairs. It is said that more than a thousand diners were fed there daily. By this time, there were three other Delmonico's thriving in New York: the original "Citadel," 22 Broad Street, and Madison Square. Altogether, the restaurants employed more than four hundred people. Certainly, Lorenzo Delmonico had a bead on contemporary entrepreneurial chefs and restaurateurs!

The late 1870s saw the return of Chef Ranhofer to the Madison Square restaurant as well as the deterioration of Lorenzo Delmonico's health. With the latter, the daily responsibilities of running the restaurants fell to Charles Delmonico, who had been well trained by his uncle. Chef Ranhofer was not only an extraordinary cook, he was also a superb manager who was more than able to meet the demands of the age of opulence and explosion of wealth that was on the horizon. Between the two men, the Delmonico empire would prosper as it catered to the whims and excesses of the newly moneyed as they preened in the ostentatious public display of extravagance and consumption.

With Lorenzo Delmonico's passing in 1881, Charles inherited the business, and he continued to run it until his untimely death in 1884. The restaurants were left to his sister Rosa and their late sister's children, Charles Delmonico Crist, Lorenzo Delmonico Crist, and Josephine Crist Otard. Charles changed his name to Charles Crist Delmonico and, along with his Aunt Rosa, continued to run the restaurants in the Delmonico style. Known as Young Charley, he was the managing director of the Delmonico businesses until 1901 and was, in the manner of his predecessors, an excellent restaurateur, skilled at both operations and hospitality.

By 1888, there were just two restaurants in the network, the original Citadel on South William Street and the opulent Madison Square establishment. The Delmonico family had been serving the citizens of New York for more than fifty years. The magnificent old Citadel had been in operation for fifty-three years and was in great need of refurbishment. Rather than renovate, young Charley chose to rebuild on the same site. In 1890, he laid the cornerstone for what would be its elegant replacement.

The new eight-story building—the new Citadel—opened a year later, more opulent than the original and, again, the talk of the town. The first floor had the signature café, along with a magnificently appointed dining room. The second floor held the ladies' dining rooms and a few other private dining rooms.

To generate income, the next five floors were set aside to be leased to outside businesses. The kitchen was relegated to the eighth floor, so one can only imagine the planning necessary to get the meals to the tables with enough speed to ensure that they remained hot.

As business demands changed, the Broad Street restaurant was closed, much to the dismay of old-timers for whom it had been a favorite watering hole for almost thirty years. Young Charley still maintained a strong leadership role with the remaining three restaurants, helped, in part, by the venerable Charles Ranhofer who was *chef de cuisine* overseeing all the kitchens. As the downtown scene lessened, the two masters had plans to bring their skills to Manhattan's elite, who had begun to settle uptown.

A spectacular new Delmonico's was opened on the northeast corner of Fifth Avenue and Forty-fourth Street in November 1897. Its grandeur surpassed all its predecessors, but it was also a source of gossip, for within its halls smoking was permitted in the dining room for the first time and an orchestra played while diners ate, another first. Until then, smoking was permitted only in cafés or private rooms, and never in the presence of ladies, and music was to be listened to, not played as background noise. Once again, the Delmonicos broke new ground.

The restaurant reflected the extraordinary opulence of the day—electric lights; Tiffany china and silver; velvets, silks, and satins; fine woods; and marble set the tone. On the first floor, there was a special restaurant overlooking Fifth Avenue reserved for ladies, allowing a view of passersby and arriving coaches. Its adjoining Palm Court had huge windows that opened the room to the world. The palatial main dining room and the café were on the second floor, decorated in the Delmonico fashion to just within the bounds of good taste.

TOP: A spectacular new Delmonico's opened on the northeast corner of Fifth Avenue and Forty-fourth Street in November 1897.

ABOVE: One of the opulent dining rooms at the original Delmonico's

There were anterooms that could be opened to unite with the larger rooms to make one gigantic banquet space. The third floor provided a ballroom, brightly electrified and generously decorated, along with private rooms and another Delmonico innovation, a "bride's room," reserved for the privacy of the stars of the many weddings that would be celebrated here. The kitchen was located in the basement, and the top floors were used for paid lodging, servants, and maintenance. All the mechanical necessities required to run this masterpiece were located in a sub-basement. The galas and balls, private dinners and feasts, and íntime affairs and liaisons that were held here fueled the gossip columns for years.

Shortly after the opening, Charles Ranhofer moved all the kitchen operations to the new location. It would operate as a central kitchen for all the external catering as well as be the focal point for the cooks in the other restaurants. This move was followed by the closing of the Madison Square restaurant, a much-maligned decision. It had been particularly popular with women, as it had been in the heart of the elite shopping district, but the lease had expired and business was moving uptown, so Charley made the appropriate economic choice to cease operation. In this same year, the Delmonico family as well as the entire restaurant community was saddened by the death of Charles Ranhofer.

ABOVE: Part of the kitchen staff

OPPOSITE: Chef Charles Ranhofer

As the century came to an end, the Delmonicos had only two restaurants, the new Citadel and the stylish Forty-fourth Street locale. Sadly, the beginning of the new century would find the Delmonico empire fading. Young Charley passed on, leaving his Aunt Rosa at the helm. Although she had been a strong backer and an interested owner, she had never been on the scene and few patrons knew her. She wisely left the day-to-day management to the staff that had worked with Charley, all of whom kept the Delmonico ethic in place.

With Rosa's death in 1904, the business was left to her niece and nephew, with her niece, Josephine, given full managerial control. This did not sit well with her nephew, who initiated a long and bitter legal dispute. After some time, it was clear that Josephine did not have the Delmonico hospitality gene, and the businesses were clearly in financial disarray. She finally gave the running of the restaurants to a longtime employee, Eugene Garnier, who managed to pull the operations out of the doldrums and raise the restaurants back to the Delmonico standards.

It is interesting to note that as Delmonico's fortunes waned, the Fortune 500 was looming on the horizon. Many of America's most powerful brokerage houses, financial institutions, and commercial businesses began to flourish as the century turned. Merrill Lynch (founded by Charles E. Merrill and Edmund C. Lynch), for instance, began operations in 1907 and, focusing on the average investor, had expanded to become Merrill, Lynch & Co. at 7 Wall Street by 1915. An associate's comments that "Merrill could imagine the possibilities, Lynch imagined what might go wrong in a malevolent world" could be equally

used to describe the early innovative partnership of the Delmonico brothers. These two entities also played a role in women's emancipation; Merrill Lynch launched the career of Wall Street's first female bond trader, Annie Grimes, just as Delmonico's had featured the first woman cashier and allowed the first public gathering of women in a restaurant.

When Garnier retired in 1910, Josephine hired a general manager named Wilfred Taupier, who began extensive renovations of the Forty-fourth Street restaurant, returning it to its glory. Telephones were installed in booths and electric fans offered a cool breeze on sultry summer days. The Delmonico innovation and quality were there; however, times were once again changing, and business was moving farther uptown. The economic health of the restaurant was not as good as its exterior would indicate. Even so, the lease was renewed for another fifteen years, forging a belief that Delmonico's Forty-fourth Street would weather any financial difficulties.

The Delmonico's code, upheld by all of its members, stated that above all else, the customer was there to be pleased and it was the job of the family to ensure this pleasure. Everything should be the best available. It was essential that the family bring immediate and personal attention to and rectification of any justified criticism about the service, meals, or wines by any guest. These rules were difficult to follow in the changing world of the twentieth century as the restaurant business became less an enjoyment for the very rich and more a convenience for the masses.

Along with the changing cultural mores, one of which was the lack of wine and spirits caused by Prohibition, came the demise of some of the American bounty upon which the Delmonicos had based their menus. Prohibition made it impossible to duplicate the rich wine-based sauces of French cuisine, and extensive wine cellars were sold off or hidden from the revenuers. Wild game was no longer sold, and many of the local, native species had all but disappeared. Farms were being turned over to development. The times had changed too quickly for the restaurateurs to keep up with.

The beloved Citadel did not make it through the First World War. Eating habits had changed, business became more harried, and the opulent restaurant setting no longer served a purpose for the movers and shakers of the financial district. The restaurant closed in 1917, and the property was sold, leaving many sad tales to be told. Most of all, historians were saddened that the Delmonico heirs could not keep the trust of the founding brothers, who bade their successors never to let the business or buildings pass from family control. With the sale of the Forty-fourth Street restaurant in 1919, the final blow was struck. The Delmonico family no longer had a presence in New York.

Although the restaurants were owned by others, by 1923 the last authentically styled Delmonico's restaurant in New York was closed. Throughout the decades, the South William Street building stood as it had been built, with the Pompeian columns at its portals and the Delmonico name in place above the doors. The original restaurant space was in use off and on, and the upper floors remained as rentals. For some time, it was known as Oscar's Delmonico's, and in 1977 it was returned to just Delmonico's Restaurant. This closed in 1992, and the building remained vacant for six years until it was purchased by the Bice Group, an Italian restaurant company, with the intent of returning the space to its former grandeur. More than a million dollars was spent to refurbish the commodious restaurant area and recreate the opulence of its days of glory. Delmonico's Restaurant at 56 Beaver Street reopened in 1998. In 1999, it was sold to the Ocinomled Partnership, led by Milan Licul.

With the purchase, it was Mr. Licul's desire that the restaurant and grill would strive to repeat the experience offered by all the esteemed Delmonico hosts. The setting is rich in woods and fine damasks. The tableware reflects the best of the past. The wine cellar is replete with valued vintages. Galas and private dinners are as joyous as they were in the days of Lorenzo, Charles, and Chef Ranhofer. Huge paintings of past celebrations cover the walls, bringing the warmth and welcome of the past to today's diners. Many of the dishes acclaimed more than a hundred years ago are on the menu, some as they originally were and others with a contemporary twist. All of this to welcome diners from around the world in the same spirit of hospitality and generosity shown by John and Peter Delmonico in their little pastry shop in 1834.

THE

# Epicurean

BY

CHARLES RANHOFER

OF

DELMONICO'S.

F.G. DIEFENBACH. DEL.

# Entertaining in the Delmonico Style

Thankfully, some things never change. Charles Ranhofer begins his introduction to *The Epicurean* by saying that "the success of a dinner depends upon good cooking, the manner in which it is served, and especially on entertaining congenial guests." However true his motto, though, the manner in which he carried it out would be difficult to translate to the contemporary table due to the financial and labor constraints of running a restaurant (or a household) in the modern world.

The Delmonico restaurants were staffed with legions of skilled professionals. Trained chefs directed the activities of more than one hundred workers in the kitchen. There were full butcher shops and elaborate pastry stations, all filled with commanding cooks and their assistants. At one point, there were as many as forty-five line cooks working the stoves to create luxurious meals for discerning Delmonico diners.

At Delmonico's, menus were created for all meals, including breakfast, but the emphasis was on those for dinners. Once women were included in restaurant affairs, the menu was usually composed of lighter dishes (although not light by today's standards) and concluded with spectacular desserts. If a meal was given in honor of a foreigner, then it had to include either dishes of the guest's nation or dishes reflecting that cuisine and named in his (it was almost always a gentleman) honor.

The menu was a symphony of color, texture, and elegance. It was advised that the kitchen vary the types and richness of the meats, offer foods at the height of their season, and feature fresh products when at all possible, with preserved ingredients used only when nothing else was available. Every guest was presented with a menu, hand-painted and printed on silk by Tiffany & Co. when the dinner was a special one.

Some of the rules of presentation were:

Oysters were almost always served first, no matter the type of service (French, Russian, or American).

OPPOSITE: The original frontis art for *The Epicurean,* published in 1894 and written by Chef Charles Ranhofer.

BELOW: Delmonico's large confectionary department

Soup—one clear and one thick—was presented after oysters.

Hors d'oeuvre, side, or light dishes came next. These might be timbales, croustades, cromesquis, palmettes, mousselines, bouchées, cannelons, or rissoles, which were always be accompanied by olives, radishes, canapés, caviar, pickled tuna fish (tunny), anchovies, or other small fresh or preserved dishes.

If fish was braised or boiled, it had to be accompanied by potatoes; if broiled or sautéed, cucumber salad; and if fried, it was served plain or with a light sauce.

Removes, or *relevés*, were the solid joints of meat—saddles of veal, mutton, lamb, venison, and antelope or beef tenderloins or middle short loins—that came next. Turkey, goose, capon, pullets, ducks, or other poultry or game birds could also be served. Either was accompanied by one or two vegetables.

Then came the entrées, the heaviest items on the menu. When preparing the menu, the heaviest entrée came first and the lightest completed this section. The heaviest entrées were cut in the kitchen to avoid carving at the table. No fish was considered an entrée, although turtle or shellfish might be. Each entrée was accompanied by garnishes and a vegetable served separately.

Punch or sherbet always followed, to refresh the palate.

Roasts were served after the refreshment. A game roast was preferred, but other meats could also be presented. If another meat was used, it was generally truffled.

Cold dishes came after the roast but before the hot dessert. They could be served with a green salad. Terrines, ballotines, and galantines were considered excellent choices.

Entremets, or hot sweet dishes such as puddings, fried creams, fritters, pancakes, omelettes, and soufflés, were next on the menu. They were followed by cold sweet dishes such as jellies, creams, charlottes, or large cakes.

And, at long last, came dessert. These were often sculpted into elaborate centerpieces made of pulled and spun sugars, pastes, and all manner of extraordinary ingredients. The presentations were followed with cheeses, fresh, candied and preserved fruits, petit fours, and bonbons.

Throughout the meal, copious amounts of wine and cordials were offered, with specific instructions on type and temperature appropriate to each course.

Dinners at Delmonico's were often ordered without limitation to décor, cost, or ingredients. The owners were held in such reverence that all details of the meal (plus entertainment) were entrusted to their excellent taste. Lorenzo was quoted as saying that the restaurant often gave "dinners that cost over $100 a head." It is said that, although the food offered could be over-the-top, it was the flourishes that took the experience to its apex; the menus might be printed in gold on silk or satin at a price of fifteen to twenty dollars each, the flowers might cost as much as twenty dollars per person, and the entertainment would frequently be the current in-demand singers and musicians, hired at their going rate.

The most famous of all Delmonico dinners was hosted by the well-known importer Edward Luckmeyer in the late 1800s. A special table seating seventy-five was constructed for the event, the center of which was a thirty-foot-long lake, complete with woodland landscaping. The lake was covered by a Tiffany-made gold mesh netting that extended to the ceiling so that it would encage the group of swans set aswimming in it. Floral hills were placed around the lake to keep the water from being splashed upon the diners—luckily, since the unhappy swans occasionally fought and, it was reported by some witnesses, even engaged in the ritual of mating. Years later, when the Vanderbilts replicated the dinner in their home, its extravagance had not diminished, and the event was again the talk of the town.

Because of both the freewheeling profligacy of the nouveau riche society and the availability of low-cost labor, these flights of fancy became almost commonplace through the end of the nineteenth century and the beginning of the twentieth. With the First World War, such extravagance ended as the sobering reality of the modern world took its toll. Not until the prosperous 1980s did New York City once again see such luxurious entertainments. With this unprecedented economic growth came a new class of entrepreneurs willing to extol their surplus wealth in a manner equal to the expansiveness of their predecessors, and America experienced a brief return to those "golden" days.

Because of the opulence long associated with the Delmonico style of dining and entertaining, throughout the centuries the name itself became synonymous with luxury. Even people who had never dined in a Delmonico establishment understood that when something was labeled "Delmonico" it was supposed to be the very best that could be offered. Consequently, many dishes, restaurants, and ingredients that have had no association with either the Delmonico family or the restaurant have come into common usage. We like to think of these as a compliment to our continued insistence on elegance, superb ingredients, fine dining, world-class wines, and, most of all, welcoming hospitality.

Delmonico's was the first New York restaurant to offer printed menus. For special events and dinners, these menus were often created by Tiffany & Co. with elaborate hand-painted silk covers and original art.

Hors-d'oeuvre, or side dishes, signifies out of the work, they having no place on the bill of fare. They are certain appetizing dishes placed on the table before dinner, remaining on in the Russian service, until dessert; in French service they pass round a few hors-d'oeuvre after the soup, such as melons, olives, radishes, celery, figs, artichokes, canapés, etc.

In Russia, the hors-d'oeuvre is highly appreciated, and as in the Russian service, the removes, entrées and roasts do not appear on the table, which should be handsomely decorated with all kinds of hors-d'oeuvre so as to make an elegant display. In formal dinners they serve in another apartment close to the dining room, a table spread with a variety of side dishes; they also serve at the same time kummel, brandy, vermouth, absinthe, gin, etc.

CHARLES RANHOFER
*The Epicurean*

# Hors d' Oeuvre

CANAPÉS À LA RANHOFER

CAVIAR PRESENTATION

CHEESE STRAWS

CLASSIC ESCARGOTS WITH
GARLIC HERB BUTTER

QUAIL EGGS BENEDICT

SHRIMP WITH ALLIGATOR PEAR MOUSSE

MINI BEEF "DELINGTONS"

# Canapés à la Ranhofer

Throughout Charles Ranhofer's reign in the Delmonico kitchen, the restaurant was the scene of hundreds of society dinners, parties, balls, entertainments, and business affairs. Because the kitchen was huge and the staff numbered in the hundreds and the budgets were seemingly unlimited, the menus were lavish and frighteningly opulent in fat, calories, and extravagance.

Canapés were often served en masse, as it would have otherwise seemed ungenerous. The base was often a rich bread that had been fried in butter, the spread a compound butter, the star foie gras, rich meats, or cheeses, and the garnish caviar or truffles. Nowadays, we have our own repertoire of canapés that are featured at the many corporate parties held at the restaurant.

# Eggplant Caviar and Herbed Goat Cheese Canapés

MAKES ABOUT 4 DOZEN

*12 thin slices whole-wheat bread, crusts removed*

*¼ cup (½ stick) melted unsalted butter*

*8 ounces soft goat cheese*

*2 tablespoons heavy cream*

*1 tablespoon minced fresh herbs (parsley, chives, marjoram, or other herb, singly or in a mix)*

*Eggplant Caviar (recipe follows)*

*10 sun-dried tomatoes, julienned*

CANAPÉS FROM LEFT TO RIGHT:
Fresh Tuna Canapés with Wasabi Caviar, Salmon and Crab Flowers, Eggplant Caviar and Herbed Goat Cheese Canapés, Westphalian Ham and Fig Canapés, Chicken Liver Mousse Canapés

Preheat the oven to 350°F.

Cut each bread slice into quarters. Using a pastry brush, lightly coat each piece of bread with the melted butter. Place the bread on a nonstick baking pan in the oven and toast, turning occasionally, for about 5 minutes, or until golden brown. Remove from the oven and place on a double layer of paper towel to cool. (The paper towel will absorb excess oil.)

Combine the goat cheese and cream in the bowl of an electric mixer fitted with the paddle. Beat on medium until soft and creamy. Fold in the herbs.

Using a small offset spatula or small knife, cover half of each toast piece with the goat cheese mixture to make a neat, even triangle. Cover the remaining triangle with Eggplant Caviar. Place a strip of sun-dried tomato on the dividing line between the two toppings. Serve immediately. (If you are feeding a small group, it is a good idea to make only 12 at a time, as the eggplant will make the toast soggy as it sits.)

## EGGPLANT CAVIAR

MAKES ABOUT 4 CUPS

*3 pounds (about 3 large) eggplant*

*3 cloves garlic*

*2 tablespoons minced fresh thyme leaves*

*¼ cup plus 3 tablespoons olive oil*

*¼ cup plus 2 tablespoons dry white wine*

*1 large onion, peeled and finely chopped*

*1 cup finely chopped peeled, cored, and seeded tomatoes*

*2 teaspoons smoked paprika*

*1 teaspoon ground coriander*

*½ teaspoon ground cumin*

*Coarse salt and freshly ground pepper to taste*

*2 tablespoons finely chopped flat-leaf parsley*

*1 teaspoon fresh lemon juice*

Wash and trim the eggplants. Cut them in half lengthwise.

Chop 2 cloves of the garlic and combine with the thyme and ¼ cup of the olive oil and ¼ cup of the wine in a nonstick baking pan large enough to hold the eggplant halves. Place the eggplants, cut sides down, into the baking pan and set aside to marinate for 1 hour.

Preheat the oven to 350°F.

Place the eggplants in the preheated oven and bake for 45 minutes, or until very tender.

Remove from the oven and set aside to cool.

When cool, using a large kitchen spoon, scrape the flesh from the skin. If necessary, finely chop the flesh.

Heat the remaining 3 tablespoons of olive oil in a large nonstick frying pan. Mince the remaining garlic clove. Add the onion and garlic and sauté for about 2 minutes or until lightly colored. Add the remaining wine and bring to a simmer. Then, add the tomatoes and cook, stirring frequently, just until the tomatoes have wilted. Add the reserved eggplant, paprika, coriander, and cumin. Season with salt and pepper and cook, stirring frequently, for about 5 additional minutes or until the mixture has dried out somewhat.

Remove from the heat and add the parsley and lemon juice. Set aside to cool. Use immediately or transfer to a container with a lid and store, tightly covered and refrigerated, for up to 1 week.

## Westphalian Ham and Fig Canapés

MAKES 24

> ¼ cup extra-virgin olive oil
>
> 1 garlic clove, peeled and sliced
>
> 6 small (4 inches by 3½ inches) slices multigrain or homemade-style white bread, crusts removed
>
> 6 ripe but firm black mission figs
>
> About ½ cup fig jam
>
> 6 thin slices (about 9 inches by 3½ inches) Westphalian ham or Serrano ham or prosciutto, halved
>
> About ¼ pound truffle cheese such as Boschetto al Tartufo Bianchetto or Sottocenere

Combine the oil and garlic in a small saucepan over medium heat. Bring to just a simmer and immediately remove from the heat. Set aside to cool slightly.

Preheat the oven to 350°F.

Using a pastry brush, lightly coat each piece of bread with the seasoned oil. Place the bread on a nonstick baking pan and bake, turning occasionally, for about 5 minutes, or until golden brown. Remove from the oven and place on a double layer of paper towel to cool. (The paper towel will absorb excess oil.)

Depending upon their size, cut each fig into sixths or more; the pieces should be small bite-sized.

Using a small offset spatula or small knife, carefully cover each piece of toast with an even layer of fig jam. Place 2 half slices of ham, slightly overlapping, over the jam on each piece.

Carefully cut each piece into quarters. Place a piece of fig in the center. Using a cheese slicer or vegetable peeler, shave off a small piece of truffle cheese, tuck it under the fig, and serve.

## Fresh Tuna Canapés with Wasabi Caviar

MAKES 4 DOZEN

*One 6-ounce center-cut, sushi-grade tuna loin,*
*about 4 inches long by 2 inches wide*

*½ cup mayonnaise*

*2 tablespoons Sriracha or other hot sauce*

*1 tablespoon fresh lemon juice*

*¼ cup extra-virgin olive oil*

*1 garlic clove, peeled and sliced*

*8 thin slices seven-grain (or other multigrain) bread, crusts removed*

*½ English or hothouse cucumber, cut into matchsticks*

*1 ounce (2 tablespoons) green (wasabi-flavored) flying fish roe*

Wrap the tuna in plastic film and place in the freezer for about 1 hour, or until very firm but not frozen.

Combine the mayonnaise, hot sauce, and lemon juice in a small mixing bowl. Cover and refrigerate until ready to use.

Combine the oil and garlic in a small saucepan over medium heat. Bring to just a simmer and immediately remove from the heat. Set aside to cool slightly.

Preheat the oven to 350°F.

Using a pastry brush, lightly coat each piece of bread with the seasoned oil. Place the bread on a nonstick baking pan and bake, turning occasionally, for about 6 minutes, or until golden brown and dry. Remove from the oven and place on a double layer of paper towel to cool. (The paper towel will absorb excess oil.)

Line a cutting board with plastic film.

Remove the tuna from the freezer and, using a mandoline or a very sharp sushi knife, cut each loin crosswise into ⅛-inch-thick slices. This should yield 9 slices. As you cut, place the tuna slices in a single layer on the cutting board. When all the slices have been cut, cover with plastic film and, using a small, heavy frying pan, gently pound down on each slice to stretch it to about 4 inches by 3 inches. Take care not to pound too hard or the slices will begin to disintegrate. When all the slices have been flattened, transfer the entire board to the refrigerator to chill for about 15 minutes.

Using a small offset spatula or small knife, evenly coat each toast slice with seasoned mayonnaise. Place one slice of tuna on each slice of bread to entirely cover.

Using a chef's knife, cut each piece in half, crosswise. Then, cut each half into thirds, lengthwise. Each slice should yield six 2-by-1-inch pieces.

Place 2 cucumber matchsticks, lengthwise on the diagonal, in neat lines on each canapé. Place a dollop of mayonnaise and caviar in between each line and serve.

## Chicken Liver Mousse Canapés

MAKES 24

*6 thin slices white bread, crusts removed*

*¼ cup olive oil*

*Coarse salt and freshly ground pepper to taste*

*1 large hard-boiled egg, peeled*

*Chicken Liver Mousse (recipe follows)*

*¼ cup finely chopped chives*

*Cracked black pepper to taste, optional*

Preheat the oven to 350°F.

Using a pastry brush, lightly coat each piece of bread with the olive oil and season with salt and pepper. Using a sharp knife, cut each slice into four equal triangles. Place the triangles on a nonstick baking pan and bake, turning occasionally, for about 6 minutes, or until golden brown and dry. Remove from the oven and place on a double layer of paper towel to cool. (The paper towel will absorb excess oil.)

Finely chop the hard-boiled egg and place it in a small bowl.

Using a small offset spatula or small knife, generously coat each toast triangle with the Chicken Liver Mousse. Then garnish each canapé with the chopped egg and chives. If desired, grate a bit of cracked pepper over each and serve immediately.

### CHICKEN LIVER MOUSSE

*2 tablespoons unsalted butter*

*1 pound chicken livers, rinsed and patted very dry*

*Coarse salt and freshly ground pepper to taste*

*3 thick slices bacon, diced*

*1 tablespoon olive oil*

*1 medium onion, peeled and diced*

*1 clove garlic, peeled and minced*

*1 cup Madeira wine*

*¼ cup white balsamic vinegar*

*Pinch ground cloves*

*Pinch freshly grated nutmeg*

*Pinch ground cinnamon*

*¼ cup finely diced smoked ham*

*½ cup whipped cream*

Heat the butter in a medium sauté pan over medium heat. Season the livers with salt and pepper and add to the hot butter. Cook, stirring occasionally, for about 5 minutes, or until nicely colored. Using a slotted spoon, transfer the livers to a plate.

Immediately add the bacon to the hot pan along with the olive oil. Fry for about 3 minutes or until the bacon has begun to render its fat and crisp slightly. Add the onion and garlic and continue to cook for another 3 minutes, or until the onions begin to take on some color.

Return the livers to the pan. Season with salt and pepper to taste, stirring to combine well. Add the Madeira, stirring to deglaze the pan. Raise the heat and bring to a simmer. Lower the heat and cook for about 10 minutes, or until the liquid has reduced by half.

Stir in the vinegar. Raise the heat and bring to a simmer. Simmer, stirring continually, for about 5 minutes or until the flavors have melded and the vinegar has evaporated slightly. Remove from the heat and set aside to cool.

When cool, scrape the mixture into the bowl of a food processor fitted with the metal blade. Process, using quick on and off turns, to make a smooth purée.

Scrape the purée into a clean bowl. Add clove, nutmeg, and cinnamon, stirring to blend well. Fold in the ham. When incorporated, fold in the whipped cream. Taste and, if necessary, adjust the seasoning.

Use immediately or store, covered and refrigerated, for up to 2 days.

## Salmon and Crab Flowers

MAKES 36

*9 large, thin slices black, rye, or pumpernickel bread, crust removed (see note)*
*3 tablespoons melted unsalted butter*
*Crab Salad (recipe follows)*
*6 thin slices smoked salmon, about 6 inches by 3½ inches, halved*
*½ cup crème fraîche*
*2 teaspoons vodka*
*1 teaspoon prepared horseradish, well-drained*
*1 teaspoon fresh lime juice*
*2 tablespoons Osetra caviar*

Preheat the oven to 350°F.

Using a pastry brush, lightly coat each piece of bread with the melted butter. Place the quarters on a nonstick baking pan and bake, turning occasionally, for about 5 minutes, or until golden brown. Remove from the oven and place on a double layer of paper towel to cool. (The paper towel will absorb excess oil.)

Using a small offset spatula or small knife, thinly coat each toast with an even layer of the crab mixture. Cover each with 2 slightly overlapping pieces of salmon.

Using a 1½-inch round, fluted cookie cutter, carefully cut 4 rounds from each piece of toast. You should have 36 flower shapes.

Combine the crème fraîche, vodka, horseradish, and lime juice in a small bowl. Whisk constantly until soft peaks form.

Using a demitasse spoon (or a pastry bag fitted with the smallest plain tip), place a dollop of the crème fraîche mixture in the center of each canapé. Again using a demitasse spoon, place a small garnish of caviar on top and serve.

NOTE: You will need to cut four 1½-inch rounds from each slice of bread, so if the slices are not big enough, you may need to use more.

## CRAB SALAD

*1 tablespoon mayonnaise*

*1 teaspoon Dijon mustard*

*1 tablespoon finely chopped chives*

*1 tablespoon finely chopped flat-leaf parsley*

*1 tablespoon finely minced red bell pepper*

*½ tablespoon finely minced red onion*

*1 tablespoon fresh lemon juice*

*½ pound Peekytoe crab or crab claw meat, cleaned and chopped*

*Coarse salt and freshly ground pepper to taste*

Combine the mayonnaise and mustard in a small mixing bowl. Stir in the chives, parsley, red pepper, and onion. Add the lemon juice, stirring to blend. Fold in the crab and season with salt and pepper. Cover and refrigerate for 1 hour.

When ready to use, taste and adjust the seasoning. Drain off any excess liquid that has accumulated in the bowl and use as directed in the recipe.

# Caviar Presentation

There seems to be no food with more royalist leanings than caviar, long associated with the most desirable Caspian Sea roe favored by Russian tsars and Iranian kings. Simply the salted eggs (roe) of several species of sturgeon, Caspian Sea caviar is classically divided into three types: beluga, osetra, and sevruga. Beluga eggs are the largest, richest, and most expensive. Osetra is a smaller roe with a pale, almost-yellow tint (it can also have other tints) and a faintly nutty flavor. The smallest egg is dark sevruga, which is saltier and more intensely flavored, although still delicate. Each type is delicious. Unfortunately, due to overfishing, piracy, war, and pollution, Caspian Sea caviar is no longer plentiful or has been banned from importation into the United States.

However, as unbelievable as it seems, at the height of Delmonico's fame, the United States was the world's largest exporter of sturgeon caviar, with most of the excess ending up as "bar food" in workingmen's taverns, where its saltiness would encourage more drinking! By the late 1800s, the abundant sturgeon in the Delaware River were producing huge amounts of caviar and knowledgeable processors were packing it almost faster than the fish could produce. At one point, it is said that the demands of the "American Caviar Rush" created the processing of more than five million pounds a year. This, of course, resulted in the depletion (and eventual extinction) of the native sturgeon population and the loss of American caviar.

Although some feel that the extravagant presentation we have come to associate with eating caviar evolved from the necessity of masking the flavor of inferior caviar, others believe it was a way to distinguish luxe from everyday. While most aficionados agree that the best way to eat caviar is with more caviar and, of course, icy cold vodka to refresh the palate between bites, the discerning Delmonico diner preferred otherwise. Along with the vodka, it was silver service, champagne, horn spoons with which to heap the caviar on a tiny, warm buckwheat blini along with all the accompaniments—minced onion, chopped egg white and egg yolk, sour cream, and minced chives that met the astute Victorian diner. It is this presentation that we offer, although, today, entrepreneurs are once again creating American caviars that can stand on their own, from Tennessee (black sturgeon) and Mississippi (paddlefish), as well as from a number of other areas. If you have the opportunity to experience them, return to the warm blini and vodka combination to experience caviar in its extravagant simplicity.

Caviar is generally served directly from its tin, which should be placed in ice to keep the roe well chilled. At Delmonico's, the tin was always placed in shaved ice packed in an elaborately decorated silver container. The most important point in service is to provide a nonreactive implement with which to serve the caviar, as reactive metals such as silver will impart a bitter note to the roe. A gold spoon, on the other hand, works just fine. Generally bone or mother-of-pearl are used, but plastic will also do.

You can make the presentation as elegant or as plain as you wish. Guests should be provided with small plates and napkins. Each of the accompaniments should be placed in identical small bowls with tiny spoons (espresso spoons are the perfect size) for serving. The blinis must be served on a warm plate. Each guest should be given one blini at a time so that the warmth of the blini will contrast with the chill of the caviar and, if you have a limited amount of caviar, you should serve it to each guest yourself. (Otherwise, a caviar lover in the group may inadvertently take more than his share and leave others wanting.) Then, the accompaniments should be offered directly.

The accompaniments should all be finely chopped. The white and yolk of one egg is sufficient for six servings. You will need about two tablespoons of minced onion and a heaping tablespoon of finely chopped chives or flat-leaf parsley. Rather than sour cream, we suggest that you use crème fraîche, a bit richer and sweeter. You will need no more than a heaping tablespoon of it. This is all based on a two-ounce jar yielding enough caviar to top twelve canapés. Of course, if you are feeling flush, there can never be too much caviar.

Although classically caviar can be served on white toast points or brioche rounds, we prefer the warm, nutty flavor of homemade buckwheat blinis (page 42). They are also wonderful as a breakfast pancake or as bread with all types of smoked fish. You can make them any size you wish, but for a caviar presentation we like them no more than one and a half inches in diameter. This recipe should yield about thirty little blinis, which can be frozen and reheated when ready to use. To reheat, place in a single layer on a nonstick baking sheet in a preheated low oven for about five minutes, or until heated through.

# BUCKWHEAT BLINIS

MAKES ABOUT 30 PANCAKES

> *1 cup milk*
>
> *½ cup heavy cream*
>
> *¼ cup (½ stick) unsalted butter*
>
> *2 tablespoons brown sugar*
>
> *2 teaspoons dry yeast*
>
> *⅔ cup unbleached white flour*
>
> *⅔ cup buckwheat flour*
>
> *1 teaspoon salt*
>
> *1 large egg white*
>
> *Clarified butter, if needed to prevent sticking*

Preheat the oven to warm or 200°F.

Combine the milk, cream, and butter in a small saucepan over medium-low heat. Heat just until the butter has melted completely. Let cool to 110°F on an instant-read thermometer. Add the sugar and yeast, stirring to combine. Let rest for 5 minutes, or until the yeast has dissolved completely.

Combine the flours with the salt in a mixing bowl. Pour the liquid ingredients into the dry ingredients, mixing to just combine. Cover with plastic film and set aside in a warm, dry spot for about 1 hour, or until doubled in bulk.

Place the egg white in a small mixing bowl and beat with a handheld mixer until soft peaks form. Fold the beaten egg white into the batter.

Heat a nonstick griddle or frying pan over medium heat.

For each blini, spoon a scant 2 tablespoons of batter into the pan, leaving space around each one to allow for spreading. Cook for about 2 minutes, or until the tops are covered in little bubbles and the bottoms are golden brown. Using a narrow offset spatula or other small implement, carefully turn each blini and brown the remaining side. (If blinis stick, brush the pan with a little clarified butter).

Transfer the blinis to a nonstick baking sheet and place in the preheated oven to keep warm while the remaining blinis are prepared.

Serve warm or store, separated by waxed paper, tightly wrapped and frozen, for up to 3 months.

# Cheese Straws

MAKES ABOUT 3 DOZEN

Probably no tidbit was served more at Delmonico's than Cheese Straws, usually as a garnish on cold dishes. They were made from a well-flavored cheese dough that was baked into ⅛-inch-round sticks all of the same length. This version, made from purchased puff pastry is far easier to execute, but just as delicious. They are extremely easy to make because they are no more than some puff pastry and cheese. They can be made in advance and stored, frozen.

> *2 sheets frozen puff pastry, thawed*
> *2 egg yolks, beaten*
> *1 cup finely grated Parmesan cheese*
> *Paprika*

Working with one sheet at a time, place the puff pastry on a lightly floured work surface and, using a rolling pin, roll it out to a neat rectangle just a bit more than ¹⁄₁₆ inch thick. Quickly transfer each sheet to a nonstick baking sheet. Cover with plastic film and refrigerate for 1 hour.

Remove the chilled dough sheets from the refrigerator and transfer them to a lightly floured work surface. Trim the edges of each to make two rectangles of the exact same size.

Using a pastry brush, lightly coat the top of each piece with the beaten egg. Generously sprinkle the cheese over the top of one of the pieces. Cover the cheese with a piece of plastic film and lightly roll the rolling pin over it to make sure that the cheese adheres to the pastry. Carefully remove the plastic film and lightly sprinkle paprika over the cheese. Place the remaining sheet of pastry, egg-washed side down, on top of the cheese. Lightly roll out to make sure that both pieces are well attached. Again, transfer to a nonstick baking sheet, cover with plastic film, and refrigerate for 1 hour.

Preheat the oven to 400°F.

Line 2 baking sheets with silicone liners or generously butter 2 baking sheets (even nonstick ones).

Remove the dough from the refrigerator and, using a pastry wheel or small knife, cut the dough into strips 4 inches long by ½ inch wide.

Working with one strip at a time, twist it into a spiral shape by holding one end down on the work surface and twisting the other. It should only take two turns to make a nicely twisted straw.

Place the twisted strips, 1 inch apart, on the prepared baking sheets and bake for about 12 minutes, or until puffed and golden.

Remove from the oven and transfer to wire racks to cool slightly before serving.

# Classic Escargots with Garlic Herb Butter

SERVES 6

Escargots are rarely seen on American menus, even on those featuring classic French food. (Although you may encounter them in authentic Chinese restaurants). They were a favorite of Charles Ranhofer, but we have never featured them on our menu, either.

However, as an experiment in historical cuisine, we began serving them as hors d'oeuvre at private events and found that they created a sensation. Everyone seemed to have heard of escargots, but few really knew what they were. Nevertheless, even the unknowing were delighted with the whole shell and tiny fork and were willing to give the rich, buttery tidbit a try. Once tasted, seconds were almost always requested.

We hope that our experience will encourage you to give them a try. For the most elegant presentation, you will need ceramic escargots dishes made with six indentations to hold the appropriate serving. And, if you want to go the distance, you can also use escargots holders and forks. However you serve them, we think that you will find them delicious.

*36 canned snails, well drained*

*2 tablespoons coarse salt, plus more to taste*

*2 tablespoons baking soda*

*1¼ cups (2½ sticks) unsalted butter, at room temperature*

*2½ tablespoons minced shallots*

*1 tablespoon minced garlic*

*1 tablespoon minced flat-leaf parsley*

*1 tablespoon Pernod or other anise-flavored liqueur*

*Freshly ground white pepper to taste*

*Crusty bread, for serving*

Rinse the snails under cold, running water. Place them in a shallow bowl along with 1 tablespoon of the salt and cold water to cover. Cover with plastic film and refrigerate for 8 hours.

Place the shells in a medium saucepan with cold water to cover by 2 inches. Add the baking soda along with 1 tablespoon of salt. Place over medium heat and bring to a boil. Lower the heat and simmer for 15 minutes. Remove from the heat and drain well. Rinse each shell under cold, running water and set, opening down, on a wire rack lined with paper towel to dry completely before filling.

Combine the butter, shallots, garlic, parsley, and Pernod in a small mixing bowl. Using a wooden spoon, work the mixture together until well-blended.

Season with salt and white pepper to taste. Set aside. (If your kitchen is warm, refrigerate until ready to use. However, the butter must be soft and pliable when you fill the snails.)

Preheat the oven to 400°F.

Remove the snails from the refrigerator and drain well. Pat each snail dry with paper towel.

Working with one at a time and using a kitchen knife, place about ½ teaspoon of the compound butter into the back of each shell. Push a snail into the butter and then fill the remaining space with butter, smoothing the top with a knife or your fingertip.

Place six escargots in each of six ovenproof ceramic escargot dishes, butter-covered side up, and bake for about 7 minutes, or just until the butter has melted and the smell is indescribably enticing.

Remove from the oven and serve piping hot along with crusty bread to absorb the aromatic butter.

NOTE: Imported, canned French snails are often sold with a bag of shells attached and are usually found at specialty food stores. Sometimes you have to buy the can and the shells separately. The shells can be used over and over again if they are well washed and dried, then stored, tightly covered, after every use.

Fresh snails are occasionally available from fine fishmongers. If you find them, they will have been farm-raised and do not require the long (5 to 7 days) period of cleaning and degorging that is traditionally used to prepare fresh wild snails. They simply need a 15-minute soak in warm water (discard any that don't peek out of their shells), followed by an hour soak in salted, cold water. Cook them in a court bouillon for about 5 minutes before proceeding with the recipe.

# Quail Eggs Benedict

MAKES 12

Although there are two versions told of the invention of Eggs Benedict, we, of course, prefer the one that names Charles Ranhofer as the creator of a new lunch dish for a loyal but demanding client, Mrs. LeGrand Benedict. However, to honor historical debate, we do have to acknowledge the tale that has the equally legendary chef, Oscar Tschirky of the Waldorf-Astoria Hotel, creating the dish based on the requirements of a hungover client, Lemuel Benedict, who suggested the combination as a cure for what ailed him.

Since we no longer serve breakfast at Delmonico's, we have created a contemporary miniature version of Eggs Benedict that can be served as an hors d'oeuvre or appetizer. And, for the convenience of modern cooks, we've chosen a blender hollandaise rather than the classic French.

> Three ¾-inch-thick slices brioche bread, crusts removed (see note)
>
> 2 tablespoons unsalted butter, at room temperature
>
> ¼ cup white vinegar
>
> 12 quail eggs
>
> ¼ pound thinly sliced Serrano (or other fine-quality) ham,
>     each slice cut into 1½-inch rounds
>
> Sea salt and freshly ground white pepper to taste
>
> Blender Hollandaise Sauce (recipe follows)
>
> ½ ounce osetra caviar
>
> 1 tablespoon fresh fines herbes mix (tarragon, flat-leaf parsley, chives, chervil)

Preheat the oven to 350°F.

Lightly coat each slice of bread with butter. Using a 1½-inch round cookie cutter, cut out 12 bread rounds. Place the rounds, buttered-side up, on a nonstick baking pan and bake, turning occasionally, for about 5 minutes or until golden brown. Remove from the oven and place on a double layer of paper towel to cool. (The paper towel will absorb excess butter.)

Fill a large, shallow bowl with cold water. Set aside.

Fill a large, shallow pan (a perfect size is a cast-iron 3-quart rondeau) with cold water. Place over high heat and add the vinegar. Bring to a simmer and, using a slotted spoon, stir to create a whirlpool.

Working with one egg at a time, very carefully break the egg into a small bowl or ramekin. Slip the whole egg into the simmering, swirling water. Simmer for about 1 minute or until the white begins to solidify and form a ball, but the egg yolk is still uncooked. You can cook no more than two eggs at a time, or you will overcook them.

Using a slotted spoon, lift the eggs from the water and carefully place them in the cold water to stop the cooking and remove any vinegar flavor.

Continue cooking the eggs in simmering water, swirling each time, until all of the eggs have been cooked. Add some ice to the cold water if it loses its chill. (The poached eggs may be kept in cold water and stored in the refrigerator for up to 8 hours.)

When ready to serve, line a baking sheet with a double layer of paper towel. Set aside.

Bring a large shallow pan of water to a simmer over medium-high heat. Using a slotted spoon, transfer the eggs, one at a time, into the simmering water and heat for about 10 seconds, or just until warm. You do not want the water to boil nor the eggs to cook. Using the slotted spoon, transfer the eggs to the paper-towel-lined baking sheet to drain.

Lay the toast rounds out in a single layer. Place a couple of rounds of ham on top of each piece of toast. Then, place an egg on top of the ham in the center of each one. Season lightly with salt and white pepper to taste. Spoon just enough Hollandaise Sauce over the top to cover without running over the sides. Garnish with a dollop of caviar and a sprinkle of herbs.

NOTE: You will need twelve 1½-inch bread rounds. Depending upon the size of each slice, you may need more than 3 slices to allow for this amount.

### BLENDER HOLLANDAISE SAUCE

*3 large, very fresh egg yolks, at room temperature*

*1 tablespoon fresh lemon juice*

*A couple drops Tabasco, or other hot sauce, or to taste*

*Salt to taste*

*½ cup very hot clarified butter*

Place the egg yolks, lemon juice, hot sauce, and salt in a blender jar. Process on high for 1 minute. With the motor running, add the butter in a steady stream. This should take about another minute, at which point the sauce should be very thick. Watch carefully, as you do not want to overprocess or the sauce will break.

If not using immediately, transfer the blender jar to a bowl of very warm water to keep the sauce warm until ready to serve. Do not use boiling or very hot water or the sauce will cook.

# Shrimp with Alligator Pear Mousse

MAKES 24

In *The Epicurean,* Charles Ranhofer made many references to the "alligator pear," or avocado, as we now know it. Although it is told that he did not introduce it to Delmonico diners until the 1890s, when avocados began being regularly imported from South America, we believe that he did, in years before that period, have access to the fruit through traders coming into the New York harbor from the West Indies. And, when it was available, Ranhofer featured it as yet another exotic food at high-priced special events and private dinners.

Since the first avocados came to Delmonico's from the Caribbean and South America, we highlight them with lime, cilantro, hot sauce, and shrimp, all tropical favorites. If you want to speed this recipe along, simply buy cooked shrimp and use any toasted bread or crisp crackers as the base.

*One 7-ounce bottle clam juice*

*2 bay leaves*

*1 lemon, halved and juiced*

*1 tablespoon peppercorns*

*2 tablespoons coarse salt, plus more to taste*

*12 raw jumbo shrimp*

*2 tablespoons extra-virgin olive oil*

*6 thin slices brioche bread, crusts removed*

*½ lime*

*Freshly ground pepper to taste*

*Alligator Pear Mousse (recipe follows)*

*2 tablespoons tobiko (flying fish roe), (see note), optional*

*24 tiny cilantro leaves, optional*

Place the clam juice, bay leaves, lemon halves and juice, peppercorns, and salt in a medium nonreactive saucepan. Add 2 cups water. Place over high heat and bring to a boil. Lower the heat and simmer for 10 minutes. Prepare an ice water bath in a bowl large enough to hold all the shrimp and place it nearby. Add the shrimp to the saucepan and return to a simmer. Do not allow the mixture to boil or the shrimp will toughen.

Cook the shrimp for about 2 minutes, or just until pink. Using a slotted spoon, transfer them from the simmering liquid into the ice water bath to cool quickly. As soon as the shrimp are cool, using the slotted spoon, transfer them to a double layer of paper towel and allow them to drain well.

Peel, devein, and remove the tails from the shrimp and, using a small, sharp knife, cut each one in half lengthwise. Place in a small bowl, cover, and refrigerate until ready to use.

Preheat the oven to 350°F.

Using a pastry brush, lightly coat each piece of bread with the olive oil. Using a sharp knife, cut each slice into four equal triangles. Place the triangles on a nonstick baking pan and bake, turning occasionally, for about 5 minutes, or until golden brown and dry. Remove from the oven and place on a double layer of paper towel to cool. (The paper towel will absorb excess oil.)

When ready to serve, remove the shrimp from the refrigerator. Uncover and season with a sprinkle of lime juice and salt and pepper.

Generously coat each brioche triangle with avocado mousse. Place a shrimp half on top and dollop just a tiny bit of mousse in the center. If using, garnish with a bit of tobiko and a small cilantro leaf and serve immediately.

Historical reports state that the alligator pear, or avocado, was introduced at Delmonico's in 1895, by Richard Harding Davis, a popular journalist and ardent customer whose ground-breaking coverage of the Spanish-American War had made him a celebrity. Harding had discovered the avocado in Venezuela, and it is believed that Charles Delmonico was so impressed with the rich flavor and creamy texture that he arranged to have regular shipments of the fruit delivered to the Delmonico kitchen.

## ALLIGATOR PEAR MOUSSE

*1 large Hass avocado*

*3 tablespoons heavy cream*

*1½ tablespoons minced cilantro*

*1 tablespoon minced red onion*

*1 tablespoon minced red bell pepper*

*1 tablespoon fresh lime juice, or to taste*

*Hot pepper sauce to taste*

*Coarse salt and freshly ground pepper to taste*

Peel, seed, and chop the avocado. Place it in a mixing bowl along with the cream, cilantro, onion, and bell pepper. Using a handheld immersion blender, blend to a smooth purée. Season with lime juice, hot sauce, and salt and pepper and process to blend.

If not using immediately, coat a piece of plastic film with lime juice and pat it down on top of the mousse. Refrigerate until ready to use or for no longer than a couple of hours or it will begin to discolor.

NOTE: Tobiko, or flying fish roe or caviar, is tiny, bright orange, salted eggs that have a very delicate flavor and pop when chewed. It is used as a garnish for sushi and sashimi and is available from some specialty food stores, Japanese markets, and through the internet.

# Mini Beef "Delingtons"

A little play on words, our take on beef Wellington is a tiny mouthful of filet mignon and mushroom duxelles that we serve in the Delmonico bar. It is one of our most popular bar foods and an elegant addition to any cocktail gathering. The use of purchased puff pastry makes this an easy-to-put-together hors d'oeuvre for home entertaining. For convenience, "Delingtons" can be frozen and baked, straight from the freezer.

> One and a half 7½-inch-by-11-inch sheets frozen puff pastry, thawed
> Two 6-ounce filet mignons
> 2 tablespoons olive oil
> 1 tablespoon unsalted butter
> Coarse salt and freshly ground pepper to taste
> 1 large egg
> 1 tablespoon milk
> Mushroom Duxelles (recipe follows)
> ⅓ cup Boursin cheese

Place the puff pastry on a lightly floured work surface and, using a rolling pin, roll it out to a neat rectangle ⅛ inch thick by 9 inches wide and 15 inches long. Using a pastry wheel, cut the pastry into forty-eight 2-inch squares. Try to work quickly, as the pastry should stay very cool.

Transfer the squares to a nonstick baking sheet. Cover with plastic film and refrigerate for 1 hour.

Using a sharp chef's knife, cut each filet in half crosswise.

Heat the oil and butter in a frying pan over medium-high heat. Season the steaks with salt and pepper to taste and place them into the hot pan. Sear, turning once, for about 20 seconds per side. The meat should be browned, but still very rare. Remove from the heat and transfer to a plate. Cover with plastic film and refrigerate for about 30 minutes, or until chilled.

When chilled, remove the meat from the refrigerator and, using a chef's knife, cut each piece into 12 cubes of equal size.

If baking immediately, preheat the oven to 425°F. Line 2 baking sheets with silicone liners or parchment paper. Otherwise, just line baking sheets small enough to fit in the freezer with plastic film or waxed paper.

Whisk the egg and milk together in a small mixing bowl. Set aside.

Remove the chilled dough squares from the refrigerator and transfer them to a lightly floured work surface. Place about ¼ teaspoon of the duxelles in the center of each pastry square. Top with a beef cube. Finally, top the beef with about ¼ teaspoon of the cheese.

Carefully fold the pastry over the filling on each square, neatly tucking in the corners. Using a pastry brush, coat the seams with a bit of the egg wash and press to hold.

As you finish each piece, place it seam side down on the prepared baking sheets. When all the "Delingtons" have been made, bake them for about 10 minutes, or until golden brown and nicely puffed. Or place them in the freezer and freeze for about 90 minutes, or until solidly frozen. Carefully transfer the frozen hors d'oeuvre to resealable plastic bags or plastic containers with lids and keep frozen for up to 1 month.

When ready to serve the frozen hors d'oeuvre, transfer to lined baking sheets and bake for 12 to 14 minutes.

Serve hot.

## MUSHROOM DUXELLES

*¼ cup olive oil*

*5 shallots, peeled and sliced*

*1 tablespoon chopped garlic*

*2 pounds mixed mushrooms, cleaned and coarsely chopped*

*Coarse salt and freshly ground pepper to taste*

*½ cup dry white wine*

*Dash light soy sauce*

*¼ cup heavy cream, at room temperature*

*3 tablespoons minced flat-leaf parsley, or other fresh herbs of choice*

*Truffle oil, optional*

Heat 2 tablespoons of the olive oil in a large sauté pan over medium heat. Add the shallots and garlic and sauté for about 5 minutes, or until soft and beginning to color. Add the remaining 2 tablespoons of oil, along with the mushrooms. Season with salt and pepper and continue to cook, stirring frequently, for about 15 minutes, or until the pan is almost dry.

Add the wine and soy sauce and continue cooking for another 5 minutes, or until the pan is dry. Stir in the cream and continue cooking for another 5 minutes, or until the pan is again almost dry.

Remove from the heat. Stir in the parsley. Taste and, if necessary, adjust the seasoning with salt and pepper. Allow to cool.

When cool, scrape the mixture into the bowl of a food processor fitted with the metal blade. Process, using quick on and off turns, to finely chop, taking care not to purée. If desired, season with a bit of truffle oil.

Scrape the mixture into a clean container. If not using immediately, cover and refrigerate for up to 2 days.

In the early Delmonico's menus, appetizers were referred to as hors d'oeuvre or side dishes, and soups were always the French *potages*. There does not seem to be any rule about service for these items. Sometimes only soup began the meal, but more often than not the first course was simply oysters on the half shelf or, occasionally, caviar. For very extravagant dinners, both oysters and caviar would be served, along with radishes, celery, olives, and small fish such as anchovies. These were followed by a *potage* and then another hot hors d'oeuvre—or two or three or more.

Oysters were everyday fare in the 1800s in New York. They were piled on chopped ice in barrooms all over the city and eaten in great quantities by hard-drinking men. It is said that Diamond Jim Brady (an immensely wealthy man-about-

# Soups and Appetizers

LOBSTER BISQUE

FRESH PEA SOUP WITH TRUFFLES

FIVE ONION SOUP

PUMPKIN SOUP WITH FOIE GRAS RAVIOLINI

CREAM OF JERUSALEM ARTICHOKE SOUP

OYSTERS DIAMOND JIM BRADY

CRISPY FRIED CLAMS WITH HEARTS
OF PALM AND CRAYFISH REMOULADE

CRAB CAKES WITH LOBSTER
CORAL MAYONNAISE

SAUTÉED FROGS' LEGS PROVENÇAL

CLASSIC STEAK TARTARE

FOIE GRAS, OXTAIL, AND CHICKEN TERRINE

ROASTED QUAIL WITH PLUM COMPOTE

town, whose penchant for jewels gave him his nickname), a Delmonico's regular, would begin every meal with dozens of raw oysters. Perhaps this was to fuel his ardor for Lillian Russell, the glamorous actress and singer who was his companion for more than forty years. There were, however, many who noted that Brady's appetite could not compare with that of the beauteous Russell, who it was said could eat like a stevedore. She was known to eat four or five dozen oysters while sipping her ever-present champagne.

Charles Ranhofer considered hors d'oeuvre or side dishes to be "appetizing dishes placed on the table before dinner" or, for formal occasions, served "in another apartment close to the dining room, a table spread with a variety of side dishes." However, his menu cards have them often listed after the soup, in which case we believe that they remained on the table throughout the dinner, serving as elaborate décor for the table.

Soups, or *potages*, were considered to be a prelude to dinner, much as they are today in a restaurant or formal dinner setting. They were designed to be light, healthy, and stimulating to the appetite (although not what contemporary diners would consider light). Soups were either lean or fat, clear or thick. Garnishes were varied and ranged from simple croutons to quenelles, chiffonades, timbales, fish roes, and almost anything the chef could fashion. For all of them, a fine broth or stock was requisite. Charles Ranhofer considered them so important to a restaurant's reputation that he personally tasted and seasoned every one.

One of America's most famous soups has historically been associated with Delmonico's. Although there are many early recipes for clam chowder, the invention of tomato-flavored Manhattan Clam Chowder has been attributed to Alessandro Filippini (1889) and Charles Ranhofer (1894), both extraordinary Delmonico's chefs. Recipes for the soup are found in both of their groundbreaking cookbooks. It really is just a simple combination of clams, potatoes, tomatoes, and parsley cooked in a clear clam broth and seasoned with fat pork, salt, and pepper—a recipe that is still commonplace throughout America today.

In the contemporary Delmonico's setting, we strive to have both our appetizers and soups be light, inviting preludes to dinner. Since these offer our first opportunity to introduce diners to the menu, we try to surprise, but not overwhelm. We emphasize shellfish, much as did the original Delmonico's, and our soups tend to follow tradition. Of course, oysters, caviar, and foie gras remain integral to our menu. And we have our own Diamond Jim Brady in the person of John Krupa (see sidebar at right) to bring a bit of excess to the scene.

John Krupa, our current embodiment of Diamond Jim Brady, is Delmonico's premier customer, so much so that we have even named a steak after him. He has been known to order Oysters Diamond Jim Brady for everyone at the bar and then dine on more than a few servings himself. A man of prodigious appetites, not only for food and wine, but for life, John can be found at the bar in the grill or at a table in the restaurant almost every night. To quote him, "From the moment I walk in the door, I feel at home. The welcome by the staff, the cozy elegance, the personal touch, all make Delmonico's my home away from home. I can't imagine that the original Delmonico brothers did it any better."

# Lobster Bisque

SERVES 6 TO 8

This is the current recipe for Lobster Bisque, not the over-the-top mix of the late 1800s. Chef Ranhofer prepared a number of lobster bisques—one was thickened with lobster meat pounded into rice, twelve hard-boiled egg yolks pounded into half a cup of butter, and lots and lots more "double" cream; another with béchamel and lobster butter. He also garnished his bisques with lobster quenelles and, occasionally, caviar. In the restaurant, we garnish with lobster meat and, in tribute to earlier times, a spoon of caviar.

There really is no such thing as a simple bisque, but if you prefer, you can serve it without the lobster garnish. The lobster meat can then be used in other recipes. There is, unfortunately, no substitute for a homemade stock.

*2 tablespoons canola oil*

*6 lobster claw shells, reserved from making Lobster Stock (recipe follows)*

*3 lobster tail shells, reserved from making Lobster Stock*

*1 large onion, peeled and diced*

*5 cloves garlic, peeled and sliced*

*2 large carrots, peeled and chopped*

*2 ribs celery, trimmed and chopped*

*2 medium leeks, well washed and chopped, with some green part*

*2 tablespoons tomato paste*

*½ cup sherry*

*½ cup brandy*

*½ cup (1 stick) unsalted butter, cut into pieces, plus additional melted butter for cooking lobster garnish*

*½ cup all-purpose flour*

*3 quarts Lobster Stock*

*1 cup bottled clam juice*

*4 cups heavy cream*

*8 sprigs tarragon*

*Coarse salt and freshly ground white pepper to taste*

*Lobster meat from claws and tails, reserved from making Lobster Stock*

*2 tablespoons minced fresh herbs such as tarragon, chives, or flat-leaf parsley, or 2 tablespoons osetra caviar, optional*

Heat the oil in a large, heavy saucepan over medium heat. Add the lobster shells along with the onion and cook, stirring frequently, for about 10 minutes, or until the onion has taken on some color and the shells are bright red. Add the garlic, carrots, celery, and leeks, stirring to combine. Cook for about 10 minutes, or until the vegetables are nicely colored and beginning to cook. Stir in the

"The ancient bisques between the years 1700 and 1750 differed greatly from our modern [1850–1890] bisques. They were more like stews than soups or potages. . . . [Bisques] must be highly seasoned, although not containing much red pepper, . . . and accompanied by small, simple garnishes."

—Charles Ranhofer

tomato paste and cook, stirring constantly, for 2 minutes.

Raise the heat and add the sherry and brandy. Boil for about 4 minutes to allow some of the alcohol to burn off. Stir in the butter and cook, stirring constantly, until the butter has melted. Stir in the flour and cook, stirring constantly, for about 4 minutes, or until the flour is well incorporated and has taken on some color.

Pour in the stock and clam juice and bring to a boil. Lower the heat and simmer for about 30 minutes or until reduced by one third.

While the soup is reducing, combine the cream and tarragon in a medium saucepan over medium heat. Bring to a simmer, lower the heat, and cook gently for about 20 minutes, or until reduced by half. Remove from the heat and pour through a fine-mesh sieve into the soup base.

Return the soup to a boil, then lower the heat and simmer for about 15 minutes, or until slightly thickened.

Remove from the heat and carefully purée in a heavy-duty blender, shells and all. This will have to be done in batches. It is a good idea to hold a kitchen towel over the top of the blender, as the mixture is hot and the shells will jump around— the force of both will push the lid up.

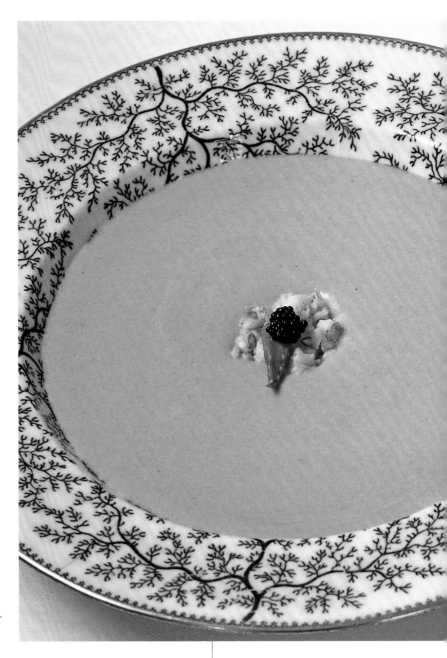

Preheat the broiler.

When all the soup has been puréed, pour it, in batches, through a fine-mesh sieve into a clean saucepan. Season with salt and white pepper. Bring to a bare simmer over medium heat.

While the soup is heating, place the meat from the lobster tails and claws in a small nonstick pan. Using a pastry brush, lightly coat each piece with melted butter. Place under the preheated broiler for about 2 minutes to just heat through. Turn off the broiler and open the door slightly so that the lobster stays warm without continuing to cook.

Ladle equal portions of the hot soup into warm, shallow soup bowls. Cut the lobster tails in half and place one piece in the center of each bowl. Lay a claw over the tail meat in each bowl and sprinkle with the chopped herbs or garnish with ½ teaspoon caviar. Serve immediately.

## LOBSTER STOCK

*Three 1½-pound live lobsters*

*2 tablespoons canola oil*

*2 ribs celery, trimmed and chopped*

*1 large carrot, peeled, trimmed, and chopped*

*1 large onion, peeled and chopped*

*3 lemons, halved*

*1 sachet containing 4 sprigs fresh thyme, 2 bay leaves, 1 teaspoon peppercorns, and 1 garlic clove*

Working one at a time, wrap each lobster in a clean kitchen towel and firmly twist off the head to separate it from the tail. (An hour in the freezer will immobilize the lobsters if you are concerned about dealing with live ones.) Twist off the claw and the knuckles. Set aside.

Using a chef's knife, cut the heads in half lengthwise. Clean out the tomalley (the greenish colored liver) and the coral (the red roe) and reserve them for use in lobster butter or mayonnaise.

Heat the oil in a large stockpot over medium heat. Add the celery, carrot, and onion and cook, stirring frequently, for about 5 minutes, or until the vegetables have sweated their liquid. Add the lemons and sachet along with 6 quarts water. Raise the heat and bring to a boil. Cook for 10 minutes.

Pack a large bowl with ice and set it aside.

Lower the heat to a simmer and add the lobster claws. Simmer for 5 minutes. Add the tails and simmer for an additional 5 minutes. Do not overcook.

Using tongs, remove the claws and the tails and immediately plunge them into the ice bath to stop the cooking. As soon as they are cool, remove them and set them aside. You don't want them to soak in the ice.

Add the lobster heads to the simmering water, raise the heat, and bring to a boil. Lower the heat and simmer for about 40 minutes, or until the liquid has reduced by half to about 3 quarts.

While the stock is simmering, carefully crack the claws open and neatly remove the meat in one piece. Crack open the tails and remove the meat. Separately reserve the lobster meat and the shells for use in the bisque.

Strain the stock through a cheesecloth-lined fine-mesh sieve into a clean container. If not using immediately, cool it in an ice bath and store, tightly covered and refrigerated, for up for 2 days, or freeze for up to 3 months.

# Fresh Pea Soup with Truffles

SERVES 6

This is a very simple soup that can be served either hot or cold. If peas are in season, by all means use fresh ones. (If so, throw some pods in for extra flavor.) If you are watching your calories and your budget, omit the cream, truffles, and truffle oil. The soup won't be as extravagant, but it will still be delicious.

*3 cups vegetable broth*

*½ cup finely chopped onion*

*½ cup finely chopped shallots*

*1 cup Riesling*

*6 cups frozen peas, thawed and well drained*

*4 fresh mint leaves*

*1 tablespoon mint chiffonade for garnish (optional)*

*Coarse salt and freshly ground white pepper to taste*

*1 tablespoon lime juice*

*½ cup heavy cream*

*1 truffle for shaving, optional*

*1 teaspoon truffle oil (see page 119)*

Combine the vegetable broth with the onion and shallots in a large saucepan over medium-high heat. Bring to a boil, then lower the heat and simmer for about 7 minutes, or until the vegetables are very soft and have infused the broth with their flavor. Add the wine and simmer for 5 minutes. Stir in the peas and mint and season with salt and white pepper. Return to a simmer and cook for 3 minutes.

Remove from the heat and process to a purée using a handheld immersion blender. (Alternatively, remove from the heat and carefully purée in a heavy-duty blender. This will have to be done in batches. It is a good idea to hold a kitchen towel over the top of the blender, as the mixture is hot and the force of the heat will push the lid up.) Add the lime juice. Taste and, if necessary, adjust the seasoning with salt and pepper.

If serving the soup cold, pour it into an ice bath to chill quickly. Stir in the cream, cover, and refrigerate for at least 1 hour to chill thoroughly.

If serving the soup hot, pour it into a clean saucepan. Add the cream and place over medium heat for about 3 minutes, or just until hot.

To serve, ladle equal portions of the soup into shallow soup bowls. Shave a few slices of white truffle over the top, if using. Drizzle with truffle oil. If using, sprinkle a few pieces of mint chiffonade around the edge of each bowl and serve.

# Five Onion Soup

SERVES 6

Because onions create a rich broth on their own without the addition of meat, onion soup has, through the centuries, been associated with poverty. This is our take on the traditional French version that, we believe, takes this humble dish to new heights and its rightful place on the elegant table.

*3 tablespoons unsalted butter*

*1 pound Vidalia or Maui onions, peeled and thinly sliced crosswise*

*1 pound sweet white onions, peeled and thinly sliced crosswise*

*1 pound leeks, white part only, well washed and diced*

*½ pound red onions, peeled and thinly sliced crosswise*

*½ pound shallots, peeled and thinly sliced crosswise*

*1 teaspoon coarse salt, plus more to taste*

*½ teaspoon light brown sugar*

*½ cup brandy*

*½ cup sherry*

*½ cup sherry vinegar, plus more to taste*

*4 cups low-sodium, fat-free beef broth*

*4 cups low-sodium, fat-free chicken broth*

*1 sachet containing 4 sprigs fresh thyme, 2 bay leaves,*
  *1 teaspoon peppercorns, and 1 garlic clove*

*Freshly ground pepper to taste*

*6 large slices white country bread, buttered and toasted*

*12 thin slices Vermont white cheddar cheese*

*¼ cup freshly grated Parmesan cheese*

Heat a large, shallow, heavy-bottom saucepan (such as a rondeau) over medium-high heat until very hot but not smoking. Add the butter, followed by the all the onions, 1 teaspoon salt, and the sugar, giving one good stir to combine and keep the bottom of the pan from burning. Cook, without stirring, for 10 minutes or until the onions begin to color on the bottom. Stir once and lower the heat. Cook, stirring occasionally, for about 25 minutes, or until the onions have begun to caramelize.

Add the brandy, sherry, and vinegar. Raise the heat and cook for 2 minutes. Add the broths and sachet and bring to a boil. Lower the heat, season with salt and pepper to taste, and simmer for 20 minutes.

Taste the soup and, if necessary, add more vinegar and salt and pepper.

Preheat the broiler.

Ladle an equal portion of soup into 6 soup crocks. Cut the toasts to fit the top of the crocks. Gently place a toast on the top of the soup in each crock. Place 2 slices cheddar cheese, slightly overlapping, on top of each crock to cover. Sprinkle an equal portion of Parmesan cheese over the top of each one.

Place the soups under the preheated broiler and broil for about 4 minutes, or until the cheese is bubbly and browned. Serve immediately.

# Pumpkin Soup with Foie Gras Raviolini

SERVES 6

This is a classically extravagant soup. It does take a bit of time to prepare, but since it makes a very elegant starter for a holiday celebration or special dinner, it is worth the effort. If you want to cut some preparation time, frozen squash purée can replace the roasted pumpkin and squash, and you could easily eliminate the raviolini. Just serve with a dollop of crème fraîche.

*One 3-pound cooking pumpkin, cut in half, seeds removed (see note)*

*One 3-pound butternut squash, cut in half lengthwise, seeds removed (see note)*

*2 tablespoons olive oil*

*Coarse salt and freshly ground pepper to taste*

*1 teaspoon ground cinnamon*

*½ teaspoon ground nutmeg*

*2 tablespoons unsalted butter*

*3 shallots, peeled and chopped*

*1 leek, white part only, well washed and chopped*

*¼ cup apple brandy*

*8 cups vegetable broth, plus more if needed*

*2 cups apple juice*

*2 medium Granny Smith apples, peeled, cored, and chopped*

*½ vanilla bean*

*2 star anise*

*1 bay leaf*

*½ cup heavy cream*

*Foie Gras Raviolini (recipe follows)*

*1 heaping tablespoon toasted pumpkin seeds*

Preheat the oven to 375°F.

Lightly coat the cut sides of the pumpkin and squash with the olive oil. Season with salt and pepper and place, cut sides down, on a baking pan lined with parchment paper. Bake for about 45 minutes, or until tender when pierced with the point of a small, sharp knife. Remove from the oven and set aside to cool.

Scrape the flesh from the pumpkin and squash into the bowl of a food processor fitted with the metal blade. Add the cinnamon and nutmeg and process to a smooth purée. Set aside.

Heat the butter in a large saucepan over medium heat. Add the shallots and leek and sauté for about 3 minutes, or just until the vegetables begin to sweat their liquid. Add the brandy, bring to a boil, and cook for about a minute, or until the pan is almost dry. Add the broth and juice, stirring to combine. Add the apples along with the reserved purée. Season with salt and pepper.

Using a small, sharp knife, slit the vanilla bean lengthwise. Scrape the seeds into the soup. (Reserve the bean to flavor sugars or drinks.) Add the star anise and bay leaf and bring to a boil. Lower the heat and simmer, stirring occasionally, for about 30 minutes, or until the apples are soft.

Remove the soup from the heat. Using a slotted spoon or tongs, remove and discard the star anise and bay leaf.

Working in batches, carefully pour the hot soup into a blender and process to a smooth purée. It is a good idea to hold a kitchen towel over the top of the blender, as the mixture is hot and the force of the heat will push the lid up.

Bring a large pot of salted water to a boil.

Pour the purée through a fine-mesh sieve into a clean saucepan. Place over medium heat. Whisk in the cream and bring to just a simmer. Taste and, if necessary, adjust the seasoning with salt and pepper. If the soup seems too thick, add a bit more vegetable broth.

While the soup is heating, drop the raviolini into the boiling water. Cook for about 2 minutes, or until they float to the top. Using a slotted spoon, scoop the raviolini from the boiling water and place on a double layer of paper towel to drain.

Ladle an equal portion of the soup into shallow soup bowls. Gently place 3 raviolini in the center of each bowl and garnish with a few pumpkin seeds.

### Foie Gras Raviolini

*1 large egg*

*18 wonton wrappers (see note)*

*6 ounces foie gras mousse (see note)*

Place the egg in a small bowl. Add 1 tablespoon water and whisk to combine. Set aside.

Lay the wonton wrappers out in a single layer on a clean work surface. Working with one at a time, place 1½ teaspoons mousse in the center of the wrapper. Using a pastry brush, lightly coat the edges with a bit of the egg wash. Fold the wrapper over the filling to make a neat triangle. Place your finger on the center of the triangle's longeset side and fold the two ends up and over your finger to make a little hat shape. Continue until you have used all the wrappers.

If not using immediately, place the raviolini on a parchment-lined baking sheet and refrigerate for up to 8 hours, or until ready to use. The raviolini may also be frozen for up to 3 months.

NOTES:

You can replace the fresh pumpkin and butternut squash with 3 cups each of canned, organic pumpkin purée and thawed frozen organic squash purée.

Wonton wrappers are available from Asian markets, specialty food stores, and some supermarkets. They are light in texture and quick and easy to use. If you can't find them, substitute prepared sheets of pasta dough cut into 3-inch squares.

Foie gras mousse is available from fine butchers, some specialty food stores, and D'Artagnan (see Sources).

# Cream of Jerusalem Artichoke Soup

SERVES 6

Although this soup is quite simple, you can take it to the Delmonico level by garnishing it with deep-fried Jerusalem artichoke slivers or artichoke leaves, roasted diced artichoke bottoms, or crumbled blue cheese. If you can't find Jerusalem artichokes, Charles Ranhofer says in *The Epicurean* to use half sweet potatoes and half artichoke hearts as a replacement.

¼ cup (½ stick) unsalted butter

4 shallots, peeled and chopped

1 leek, white part only, well washed and chopped

2 pounds Jerusalem artichokes (sunchokes), peeled and diced (see note)

2 medium potatoes, peeled and diced

2 cups finely diced celery root

3 tablespoons grated fresh ginger

¼ cup sherry

2 tablespoons all-purpose flour

8 cups chicken stock or low-sodium fat-free chicken broth

½ teaspoon ground nutmeg

Coarse salt and freshly ground pepper to taste

2 teaspoons honey, or to taste

1 cup heavy cream

4 sprigs thyme

¼ cup toasted slivered almonds

Heat the butter in a medium saucepan over medium heat. Add the shallots and leek and sauté for about 7 minutes, or just until the vegetables have begun to sweat their liquid. Add the Jerusalem artichokes, potatoes, celery root, and ginger, stirring to combine. Cover, lower the heat, and cook for about 10 minutes, or until the vegetables have all sweated their liquid and taken on just a hint of color.

Add the sherry and cook for about 3 minutes, or until the alcohol has burned off slightly. Stir in the flour. When it is completely blended into the vegetables, add the broth. Season with the nutmeg and salt and pepper. Cover and simmer for about 20 minutes, or until the vegetables begin to disintegrate. Stir in the honey.

While the soup is cooking, place the cream in a small, heavy saucepan over medium heat. Add the thyme and bring to a bare simmer. Cook gently for about 5 minutes, or until the cream has reduced by half. Remove from the heat and set aside.

Remove the soup from the heat. Working in batches, carefully pour the hot soup into a blender and process to a smooth purée. It is a good idea to hold a kitchen towel over the top of the blender, as the mixture is hot and the force of the heat will push the lid up.

Pour the purée through a fine-mesh sieve into a clean saucepan. Place over medium heat. Remove the thyme from the cream and whisk the cream into the purée. Bring to just a simmer. Taste and, if necessary, adjust the seasoning with salt and pepper.

Ladle the soup into shallow soup bowls, sprinkle with toasted almond slivers, and serve.

NOTE: Jerusalem artichokes aren't actually artichokes, but are the tuber of a particular type of sunflower. It is said that the word *Jerusalem* comes from *girasole,* the Italian word for sunflower. Their creamy flesh has a wonderfully sweet, nutty flavor. They can be eaten raw or cooked, peeled or unpeeled.

# Oysters Diamond Jim Brady

SERVES 6

This is very much a contemporary recipe, which we have named after Diamond Jim Brady, that famous bon vivant of the Gilded Age who always began his meal with oysters. We thought this would be a terrific way to honor him. This recipe highlights the oyster, but also has an extremely rich topping that we think would have been a most welcome addition to Diamond Jim's extravagant dining habits.

This is a wonderful dinner party recipe, as both the topping and sauce can be made in advance and the oysters don't take long to prepare. To bake and serve them as we do, you will need rock salt to line the baking sheet and plates. This is not necessary, but it does serve to keep the oysters steady, retaining the liquor and keeping the topping intact.

*18 oysters in the shell*
*Smoked Bacon Topping (recipe follows)*
*Béarnaise Sauce (recipe follows)*

Diamond Jim Brady

Preheat the oven to 425°F.

Line a baking sheet with rock salt. Set aside.

Line 6 luncheon plates with rock salt. Set aside.

Shuck the oysters, taking care that the deepest shell is in the palm of your hand as you open them. This will ensure that more of the liquid will be retained than if the flatter side is down. Using a small, sharp knife, loosen each oyster from its shell. Nestle the oysters in their bottom shell into the rock salt in the baking pan.

Spoon an equal portion of topping onto each oyster. Place ½ teaspoon sauce over the topping. Bake for about 8 minutes, or until the topping is bubbling and the sauce is lightly browned.

Remove from the oven and carefully nestle 3 hot oysters on each rock salt–lined plate, placing them equidistant from one another. Serve immediately.

## SMOKED BACON TOPPING

*¾ cup minced smoked bacon*

*½ cup minced shallots*

*3 tablespoons Pernod or other anise-flavored liqueur*

*½ cup minced peeled, seeded fresh tomato*

*6 tablespoons crème fraîche*

*Sea salt and fresh cracked black pepper to taste*

Place the bacon in a small frying pan over medium heat. Fry, stirring frequently, for about 5 minutes, or until crisp and brown. Add the shallots and continue to fry, stirring frequently, for about 4 minutes, or until the shallots are translucent. Add the Pernod, stirring to deglaze the pan, loosening any browned bits from the bottom of the pan with a wooden spoon.

Remove from the heat and pour through a fine-mesh sieve, discarding the liquid. Place the bacon mixture onto a clean cloth (napkin or towel) to drain completely.

When well drained, transfer the bacon mixture to a small mixing bowl. Stir in the tomato. Fold in the crème fraîche. Season with salt and pepper. The mixture may be used immediately or stored, covered and refrigerated, for 24 hours.

## BÈARNAISE SAUCE

*Juice of 1 lemon*

*½ cup champagne vinegar*

*3 stems fresh tarragon*

*1 tablespoon minced shallots*

*3 large egg yolks, at room temperature*

*1 teaspoon water*

*½ cup (1 stick) melted unsalted butter*

*1 teaspoon Delmonico's Original Steak Sauce or Worcestershire sauce*

*2 tablespoons minced fresh tarragon*

*¼ teaspoon coarse salt or to taste*

*⅛ teaspoon freshly ground white pepper or to taste*

Combine the lemon juice and vinegar in a small, nonreactive saucepan. Add the tarragon stems and shallots and place over medium heat. Bring to a simmer and simmer for about 5 minutes or until the liquid has reduced to 2 tablespoons. Remove from the heat and set aside to cool to room temperature.

When the liquid is cool, strain through a fine mesh sieve into a clean bowl. Set aside.

Place a small saucepan of water over high heat and bring to a simmer. Lower the heat to maintain a bare simmer.

Combine the egg yolks and water in a small stainless steel bowl large enough to comfortably rest in the saucepan of simmering water without the bottom of the bowl touching the water. Place the bowl over the simmering water and begin beating with a wire whisk. Continue whisking for about 5 minutes or until the mixture begins to form ribbons when the whisk is lifted.

Whisking constantly add the alternately add the butter and the reserved reduced vinegar mixture, in a slow, steady stream. When the butter is completely incorporated and the mixture is pale yellow and thick, whisk in steak sauce, followed by the minced tarragon. Season with salt and pepper to taste. Serve immediately or cover the top with a piece of plastic film to keep a skin from forming and keep warm over hot water until ready to serve.

# Crispy Fried Clams with Hearts of Palm and Crayfish Remoulade

SERVES 6

In the glory days of the Delmonico kitchen, fried clams were served in a beautifully folded napkin and garnished with fried parsley (see note), something contemporary American chefs thought they had invented in the 1990s. The early recipe for breading and frying is much the same as the one we use today, the exception being the modern inclusion of Japanese panko bread crumbs, which result in a crispier texture and more golden color.

> *30 clams, shucked, shells reserved*
>
> *1 cup Wondra flour (see note)*
>
> *2 large eggs*
>
> *2 tablespoons milk*
>
> *2 cups bread crumbs, preferably panko (see note)*
>
> *Coarse salt and freshly ground pepper to taste*
>
> *6 cups vegetable oil, for frying*
>
> *Hearts of Palm Salad (recipe follows)*
>
> *Crayfish Remoulade (recipe follows)*
>
> *30 tiny fried parsley sprigs or celery leaves for garnish, optional*

Line a baking sheet with parchment paper. Set aside.

Scrub the clam shells with a wire brush and rinse well. Pat dry.

Line 6 salad plates with seaweed, rock salt, or chopped greens. Carefully nestle 5 clam shells in an identical pattern on each plate. Set aside.

Place the flour in a resealable plastic bag. Combine the eggs and milk in a small bowl and whisk vigorously to blend well. Place the bread crumbs in a shallow bowl. Season with salt and pepper.

Working with one piece at a time, drop the clams into the flour, shaking to coat. Then dip them into the egg mixture and allow any excess egg to drip off. Finally, roll the clams in the seasoned bread crumbs. Place the finished clams on the prepared baking sheet. (Clams may now be stored, covered and refrigerated, for up to 8 hours.)

Heat the oil in a deep-fat fryer over high heat until the temperature reaches 375°F on a deep-fry thermometer.

Drop the clams, a few at a time, into the hot fat and fry for about 3 minutes, or until crisp and golden. Using a slotted spoon, transfer the fried clams to a double layer of paper towel to drain.

Spoon about 2 tablespoons of the hearts of palm mixture into each of the clam shells. Place a fried clam on top of each shell and spoon a dollop of remoulade on each one. Garnish with fried parsley. Serve immediately.

## HEARTS OF PALM SALAD

*1½ teaspoons canola oil*

*½ cup finely diced celery*

*½ cup finely diced carrots*

*½ cup finely diced leeks*

*½ teaspoon minced garlic*

*Two 14.4-ounce cans hearts of palm, well drained*

*Juice of 3 limes*

*½ cup freshly squeezed orange juice*

*3 tablespoons white wine vinegar*

*2 tablespoons Grand Marnier*

*½ cup light olive oil*

*Coarse salt and freshly ground pepper to taste*

*Hot pepper sauce to taste, optional*

*2 tablespoons chopped fresh mint leaves*

Heat the oil in a small sauté pan over medium heat. Add the celery, carrots, leeks, and garlic and sauté for about 1 minute, or just until softened slightly. Remove from the heat and transfer to a mixing bowl. Set aside to cool.

Slice the hearts of palm thinly crosswise and add, tossing to blend.

Add the lime juice, orange juice, vinegar, and Grand Marnier, stirring to combine. Add the olive oil and season with salt, pepper, and hot sauce. Cover and refrigerate for at least 2 hours or up to 8 hours before serving.

Just before serving, toss in the mint.

# CRAYFISH REMOULADE

*½ pound cooked crayfish meat, finely minced*

*1 cup mayonnaise*

*Juice and zest of 1 lemon*

*2 tablespoons minced red bell pepper*

*1 tablespoon minced red onion*

*1 tablespoon minced flat-leaf parsley*

*Hot pepper sauce to taste*

*Coarse salt and freshly ground pepper to taste*

Combine the crayfish with the mayonnaise in a small mixing bowl. Add the lemon juice and zest, bell pepper, onion, and parsley, stirring to combine. Season with hot pepper sauce, salt, and pepper.

If not using immediately, cover and refrigerate for up to 4 hours.

**NOTES:**

To make fried parsley sprigs or celery leaves, simply drop clean, dry sprigs of curly parsley or tiny celery leaves into the very hot oil in your fryer for about 20 seconds. They will immediately turn dark and crisp. Drain well on a double layer of paper towels, season with salt, and serve as a garnish.

Wondra flour is an extra-fine flour that lightly coats an ingredient. It is available from supermarkets.

Japanese panko bread crumbs are coarser than the more familiar American bread crumbs. They are available from some supermarkets, specialty food stores, and Asian markets.

# Crab Cakes with Lobster Coral Mayonnaise

SERVES 6

Almost all the early recipes for crab that we found used either whole hard-shell or soft-shell crabs. Apparently, crab cakes as we know them were not popularized until the 1930 World's Fair, where they were introduced as Baltimore Crab Cakes. Up until that time, crab cakes seem to have been a Southern specialty. Today they are found on all types of menus. We think ours, made up almost entirely of crab, is the best.

*1 tablespoon unsalted butter*

*¼ cup very finely diced red onion*

*¼ cup finely diced red bell pepper*

*1 large egg, beaten*

*Juice and zest of 2 lemons*

*1 cup mayonnaise*

*2 tablespoons Dijon mustard*

*1 teaspoon hot pepper sauce*

*1 teaspoon paprika*

*1 teaspoon cayenne pepper, plus additional to taste*

*2 tablespoons chopped chives, plus additional for garnish*

*1 pound lump crab meat, picked clean of any shell and membrane*

*1 pound colossal crab meat, picked clean of any shell and membrane*

*Coarse salt and freshly ground pepper to taste*

*1-pound bag panko bread crumbs (see page 75)*

*2 tablespoons minced flat-leaf parsley*

*½ cup clarified butter*

*Lobster Coral Remoulade (recipe follows)*

Heat the butter in a small sauté pan over medium heat. Add the onion and red pepper and sauté for about 2 minutes, or just until softened slightly. Remove from the heat and allow to cool.

Preheat the oven to 375°F.

Place the beaten egg in a medium mixing bowl. Whisk in the lemon juice and zest. Add the mayonnaise, mustard, hot pepper sauce, paprika, and cayenne, whisking to blend well. Add the chives, along with the cooled onion and red pepper, whisking to blend.

Add the lump crab meat, tossing to just blend. Add the colossal crab meat, season with salt and pepper, and very gently toss to combine. Do not mush the crab—you want large chunks to remain.

Sprinkle 1 cup of the bread crumbs over the top and very gently fold them in.

Carefully form the crab mixture into 12 small cakes of equal size. (This can easily be done with a small ice cream scoop.)

Place the remaining panko, along with the parsley, in a large, shallow bowl. Season with salt and cayenne to taste.

Carefully roll each cake in the seasoned panko, gently pressing to adhere the bread crumbs to the crab.

Heat the clarified butter in a large, ovenproof sauté pan over medium heat. Add the crab cakes and fry, turning once, for about 2 minutes, or until nicely colored. Transfer the pan to the preheated oven and bake for about 5 minutes or until hot in the center.

Remove the crab cakes from the oven and transfer them to a double layer of paper towel to drain.

Place 2 crab cakes on each luncheon plate. Drizzle the remoulade over the top and around the edge of the plate. Sprinkle with chopped chives and serve.

### LOBSTER CORAL MAYONNAISE

> *2 tablespoons cooked lobster coral (roe), finely chopped*
>
> *2 tablespoons cooked lobster tomalley (green liver), finely chopped*
>
> *1 cup mayonnaise*
>
> *2 tablespoons fresh lemon juice*
>
> *1 tablespoon finely minced capers*
>
> *2 tablespoons finely minced cornichons (see note), (or other small sour pickles)*
>
> *½ tablespoon prepared horseradish, well drained*
>
> *Hot pepper sauce to taste*
>
> *2 tablespoons chopped flat-leaf parsley*

Combine the coral and tomalley in a small mixing bowl, tossing to combine.

Add the mayonnaise, lemon juice, capers, cornichons, and horseradish, stirring to combine. Season with hot pepper sauce. Cover and refrigerate until ready to use, but for no more than 4 hours.

Just before serving, fold in the parsley.

NOTE: *Cornichon* is the French term for gherkin, or small cucumber. They are tiny, slightly sour pickles served with terrines and pâtés, available from specialty food stores and some supermarkets.

# Sautéed Frogs' Legs Provençal

SERVES 6

A classic recipe, simply executed. Our persillade (*persil* is French for parsley) sauce is a simplified version of Chef Alessandro Filippini's (see note), which calls for four hard-boiled egg yolks pounded into mustard, as well as chervil and tarragon added with the parsley.

If you want to turn this dish into a fancy appetizer, serve six legs on top of a light risotto, garnished with fried parsley (see page 75), or on a small frisée salad.

> 2 large lemons, preferably organic, well washed
>
> 18 pairs frogs' legs
>
> ½ cup olive oil, plus up to 2 tablespoons more, if needed
>
> 1 bunch flat-leaf parsley, well washed
>
> 3 cloves garlic, peeled and minced
>
> 1 cup all-purpose flour
>
> Coarse salt and freshly ground pepper to taste

Zest the 2 lemons. Separately juice each lemon, reserving the juice from each one in a separate bowl.

Rinse the frogs' legs under cold running water. Pat dry. Place the legs in a large, shallow baking dish. Add ¼ cup of the olive oil, along with the juice of 1 lemon. Toss to coat each leg, cover with plastic film, and set aside to marinate for 1 hour.

Place the parsley in a small mixing bowl. Add the garlic, along with the reserved lemon zest. Cover and refrigerate until ready to use.

Place the flour, along with salt and pepper to taste, in a resealable plastic bag.

Remove the frogs' legs from the marinade and, using paper towels, pat them dry. Working with a few at a time, place the legs in the seasoned flour, seal the bag, and shake to coat the legs well. Remove the legs from the flour and continue dredging until all of the legs are coated.

Heat the remaining oil in a large sauté pan over medium-high heat. Add the frogs' legs, in batches if necessary, and fry, turning once, for about 8 minutes, or until golden. Remove from the pan to a double layer of paper towel to drain.

When well drained, transfer to a warm serving platter. If necessary, again season with salt and pepper.

When all the legs have been fried, scrape the parsley mix into the hot pan, stirring to just heat. If necessary, add no more than 2 tablespoons of olive oil to moisten the mix. Pour the persillade over the frogs' legs and serve.

NOTE: Chef Alessandro Filippini was a renowned Delmonico's chef who was equal to Charles Ranhofer in experience and skill. He worked for the Delmonico family in many of their restaurants as manager and chef de cuisine for at least twenty-five years beginning in 1849. He wrote a number of estimable cookbooks and was one of the first authors to give the home cook an exact measurement for every ingredient in a recipe.

Charles Ranhofer tells us that frogs' legs are "less nourishing than any other animal . . . considered quite a delicacy, and healthy and agreeable to the taste. Refreshing broths are made with frogs' legs, analogous to those composed of chicken or veal."

# Classic Steak Tartare

SERVES 6

Of all the classic recipes that have gone by the wayside, steak tartare might be the leader of the pack. We would guess that a combination of fear of eating raw meat and raw eggs and the disappearance of tableside waiter service have been the cause, as the dish was not usually made at home.

Superb meat and absolutely farm-fresh eggs are, of course, required to make the perfect mix. It is essential to the dish that the meat be pristine, with no fat or membrane (think well-trimmed filet mignon) and that it be chopped just before being used. Although you can process the raw meat through a meat grinder attachment on a standing electric mixer or even in a food processor fitted with the metal blade, it is best done by hand to ensure the desired tiny cubes of bright red meat.

The classic way to serve steak tartare is to present the meat with all of the "add-ins" on the side and then mix them together tableside. To do this, plate the meat, place an egg yolk in the indentation, and garnish each plate with a selection of the "add-ins"—both those mixed in and those served on the side. Since contemporary mores make serving the finished dish more inviting, we have you mix it in the kitchen.

*16 anchovy filets, well drained*

*½ cup finely minced sweet onion*

*¼ cup minced capers*

*1 tablespoon finely minced cornichons (see page 77)*

*1½ pounds beef tenderloin, trimmed of any fat and membrane, very finely minced and well chilled*

*2 large farm fresh egg yolks*

*2 tablespoons chopped flat-leaf parsley*

*Worcestershire sauce to taste*

*Hot pepper sauce to taste*

*Coarse salt and freshly ground pepper to taste*

*6 slices brioche or homestyle white bread, toasted, crusts removed, and each cut into 4 triangles*

*2 hard-boiled egg yolks, minced*

*2 hard-boiled egg whites, minced*

*2 tablespoons Dijon mustard*

*2 tablespoons minced red onion*

Finely mince 4 of the anchovy filets and set aside. Place the remaining 12 on a plate, cover, and refrigerate.

Combine the minced anchovies, sweet onion, capers, and cornichons in a small bowl. Set aside.

Place the meat in a mixing bowl. Add the egg yolks, along with the reserved onion mixture. Add 1½ teaspoon parsley, season with Worcestershire sauce, hot sauce, and salt and pepper, and, using a kitchen fork, gently toss to mix. Work very quickly, as you want the meat to remain chilled.

Carefully transfer an equal portion of seasoned meat mixture to each of 6 luncheon plates. Place 4 toast points around the meat in the 12, 3, 6, and 9 o'clock positions. Spoon a small mound of chopped egg yolk, chopped egg white, Dijon mustard, and red onion in between the toast points.

Remove the anchovy filets from the refrigerator. Criss-cross 2 filets on top of each tartare and serve.

# Foie Gras, Oxtail, and Chicken Terrine

MAKES ONE 9-BY-3-BY-2¾-INCH TERRINE

This is our over-the-top tribute to the Victorian kitchen. We know that the staff in the Delmonico's kitchens numbered in the hundreds, so dishes such as this one would have been easy to create. We are more than aware that it is complicated and time-consuming, but sometimes a home cook just has to bite the bullet and pull out all the stops. This recipe serves that purpose. And it is a wonderfully delicious and unusual terrine that will bring hurrahs your way!

However, don't hesitate to tackle the terrines one at a time—each of them has its own individual flavor and could easily be served on its own with the traditional garnishes as a first course or as a wonderful addition to a picnic basket or a buffet table. Once you master each one, it will be a cinch to put them all together.

> 1 pound boneless, skinless chicken breasts
>
> 1 cup white wine
>
> 3 tablespoons olive oil
>
> 3 cloves garlic, peeled and sliced
>
> 6 sprigs thyme
>
> 2 dried bay leaves
>
> 1 teaspoon black peppercorns
>
> Coarse salt and freshly ground pepper to taste
>
> 20 slices bacon
>
> Eight ½-inch-thick slices Oxtail Terrine (recipe follows)
>
> 18 large fresh spinach leaves, well washed, dried, and stems removed
>
> 3 large carrots, peeled, trimmed, and cut into julienne
>
> 4 large ribs celery, peeled, trimmed, and cut into julienne
>
> 4 salsify, peeled, trimmed, cut into julienne, and blanched
>
> 2 cups warm Savory Aspic (recipe follows)
>
> Foie Gras Terrine (recipe follows)
>
> 5 fresh bay leaves

Using a chef's knife, carefully cut the chicken breast into very thin cutlets. Place the chicken in a shallow glass baking dish.

Combine the wine, oil, garlic, 3 of the thyme sprigs, the dried bay leaves, and the peppercorns and pour the mixture over the chicken. Cover the dish with plastic film and refrigerate for 1 hour.

Preheat the broiler.

Remove the chicken from the marinade and pat dry. Season with salt and pepper and place on a nonstick broiler pan. Broil, turning once, for about 2 minutes, or until just cooked through. Set aside to cool.

When cool, cut the chicken into small rectangles and set aside.

Preheat the oven to 375°F.

Line the bottom and sides of a 9-by-3-by-2¾-inch terrine with the bacon, taking care that the entire mold is covered.

Lay 4 slices of the Oxtail Terrine in an even layer on the bottom of the terrine, taking care to cover the bottom completely—cut the slices to fit, if necessary.

Place 6 spinach leaves in a thin layer over the oxtail. Lightly season with salt and pepper. Add a thin, even layer of carrots, then celery, and finally salsify, lightly seasoning each layer as you go.

Pour ¼ cup of the aspic over all.

Place a layer of chicken over the vegetables and lightly season. Repeat the layering of spinach, carrots, celery, and salsify, lightly seasoning each layer with salt and pepper as you go. Add another ¼ cup of aspic. Add a second layer of chicken and repeat the vegetable layers, ending with salsify and seasoning lightly as you go. Pour an additional ¼ cup of aspic over all.

Using all of the slices of the Foie Gras Terrine, create a thick layer of foie gras, cutting the slices to fit them in compactly.

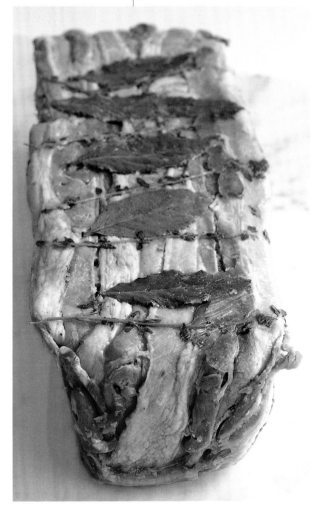

Add the final layers of spinach, carrots, celery, and salsify, lightly seasoning each layer as you go. Cover with another ¼ cup of the aspic.

Arrange the remaining 4 slices of Oxtail Terrine neatly over the entire top, cutting the slices to fit, if necessary. Pour on ¼ cup of aspic.

Place the remaining thyme sprigs and bay leaves over the top in a decorative pattern. Cover the entire terrine with a tight seal of aluminum foil. Place the sealed terrine in a baking dish large enough to hold it with a couple of inches of space around the outside. Place the baking dish in the preheated oven. Carefully add enough lukewarm water to come at least halfway up the sides of the terrine.

Bake for 15 minutes, then lower the oven temperature to 325°F. Bake for an additional 15 minutes, or until an instant-read thermometer registers no more than 128°F. Do not bake any longer or the terrine will begin to dry out. Prepare an ice bath in a bowl large enough to hold the terrine.

Remove the terrine from the oven, unwrap it, and immediately place it in the ice bath to cool quickly. Add ¼ cup of the remaining aspic, a few tablespoonsful at a time, until it is absorbed into the terrine. When the terrine has cooled, pour the remaining aspic over the top to seal it. Cover the entire terrine with plastic film.

Place another loaf-type pan or a small piece of firm cardboard cut to fit into the top of the terrine over the film. Place a 3-pound weight on top of the terrine to compact it. (Large cans of pumpkin or tomatoes work well for this purpose.) Refrigerate for at least 8 hours or up to 2 days before unmolding.

When ready to serve, unwrap and unmold the entire terrine. If it doesn't fall out easily when inverted, wrap a hot towel around it for a minute or two. It should fall right out.

Place the terrine on a serving platter with the herb-decorated top facing up. Slice the terrine, crosswise, into thin slices. Serve with cornichons (see page 77), grain mustard, pickled pearl onions, and thin toast points or crackers on the side.

## OXTAIL TERRINE

*3 large oxtails (about 9 pounds), cut into 2-inch pieces*

*4 cups dry red wine*

*5 shallots, peeled and sliced*

*3 bay leaves*

*2 tablespoons black peppercorns*

*Coarse salt and freshly ground pepper to taste*

*½ cup Wondra flour (see page 00)*

*¼ cup canola oil*

*6 cups veal stock*

*4 ribs celery, washed, trimmed, and peeled*

*2 large carrots, peeled and trimmed*

*Unsalted butter for the terrine*

*¾ cup warm Savory Aspic (recipe follows)*

Using a small, sharp knife, carefully remove all fat and sinew from the oxtails. Place the cleaned oxtails in a large shallow glass dish.

Combine the wine, shallots, bay leaves, and peppercorns and pour the mixture over the oxtail. Cover with plastic film and refrigerate for 8 hours or overnight.

Remove the oxtails from the marinade, pat dry, and set aside.

Strain the marinade through a fine-mesh sieve, discarding the solids. Reserve the liquid to use for the braising of the oxtails.

Preheat the oven to 350°F.

Season the oxtails with salt and pepper, then lightly dust them with the flour.

Place the oil in a large, shallow braising pot such as a rondeau over medium heat. When the oil is very hot but not smoking, add the seasoned oxtails. Sear, turning occasionally, until well browned on all sides.

Remove the oxtails from the pan and carefully pour off the excess oil. Return the pan to medium-high heat. Add the oxtails and the reserved marinating liquid and bring to a boil. Lower the heat and simmer for about 20 minutes, or until the liquid is reduced by half. Add the stock, celery, and carrots. Season with salt and pepper, cover, and transfer the pot to the preheated oven. Braise for 1 hour, then remove and reserve the celery and carrot. Return the oxtails to the oven and continue to braise for about 1½ hours, or until the meat is falling off of the bone.

Cut the reserved celery and carrots into a very small dice. Set aside.

Remove the oxtails from the braising liquid and place them in a shallow pan. Add about ¼ cup of the braising liquid to moisten and set aside to cool.

Generously butter the interior of a 9-by-3-by-2¾-inch terrine. Set aside.

When the oxtails are cool, carefully pick all the meat from the bones. Press enough of the oxtail meat into the buttered terrine to fill it halfway. Press an even layer of the reserved diced celery and carrots into the meat. Pack the remaining space with more oxtail meat, pressing firmly to tamp it down.

Pour ½ cup of the aspic over the top of the terrine. Let it rest for about 5 minutes to allow the liquid to be absorbed into the meat. Pour the remaining ½ cup aspic over the terrine, tapping the terrine against the work surface to encourage absorption. Wrap the entire terrine in plastic film.

Place the terrine in the refrigerator. Place another loaf-type pan or a small piece of firm cardboard cut to fit into the top of the terrine over the film. Place a 3-pound weight on top of the terrine to compact it. (Large cans of pumpkin or tomatoes work well for this purpose.) Refrigerate for at least 24 hours (or up to 2 days) before unmolding.

When ready to use, unwrap and unmold the entire terrine. If it doesn't fall out easily when inverted, wrap a hot towel around it for a minute or two. It should fall right out. Use as directed in the recipe or serve the terrine on its own with the same garnishes used for the complete terrine.

### Savory Aspic

*2 tablespoons unflavored gelatin*

*3 cups hot unsalted, fat-free chicken broth*

*Coarse salt to taste*

*¼ cup Madeira*

Combine the gelatin with ¼ cup cold water in a small bowl. Set aside for about 5 minutes, or until the gelatin has bloomed and softened. Stir in ¼ cup of the hot broth along with salt to taste. When the gelatin has dissolved, add the remaining broth and the wine. Use as directed in the above recipe.

If the aspic begins to set before used, place the bowl in a larger bowl of very hot water to melt it.

### FOIE GRAS TERRINE

½ cup Port wine

¼ cup dry white wine

¼ cup Madeira

¼ cup cognac

¼ cup coarse salt

1 tablespoon sugar

1 teaspoon freshly ground white pepper

1 teaspoon sel rose (pink salt, see note)

1 teaspoon freshly grated nutmeg

1 Grade B lobe (approximately 1 pound, 10 ounces) fresh foie gras (see note)

Combine the port, white wine, Madeira, and cognac. Set aside.

Combine the coarse salt, sugar, white pepper, sel rose, and nutmeg and set aside.

Carefully following the seam on the foie gras, open it up and, using your fingertips, pull out all the veins and sinew. You might want to wear rubber gloves to accomplish this.

*Dining at Delmonico's*

Once the lobe is cleaned, season it well with the salt mixture. Place it in a glass baking dish and sprinkle with the port mixture. Cover with plastic film and refrigerate for 8 hours or overnight.

Preheat the oven to 325°F.

Remove the foie gras from the refrigerator and drain well.

Place the foie gras in a 5¾-by-5½-by-3-inch terrine, pushing down to form the liver evenly into the terrine.

Tightly enclose the entire terrine with aluminum foil. Place the sealed terrine in a baking dish large enough to hold it with a couple of inches of space around the outside. Place the baking dish in the preheated oven. Carefully add enough lukewarm water to come at least halfway up the sides of the terrine. Bake for about 15 minutes, or until an instant-read thermometer inserted into the center reads 100°F. Do not overbake. Prepare an ice bath in a bowl large enough to hold the terrine.

Remove the terrine from the oven, unwrap it, and immediately place it in the ice bath to cool. When the terrine has cooled, remove it from the ice bath and pat dry. Cover the entire terrine with plastic film.

Place another loaf-type pan or a small piece of firm cardboard cut to fit into the top of the terrine over the film. Place a 3-pound weight on top of the terrine to compact it. (Large cans of pumpkin or tomatoes work well for this purpose.) Refrigerate for at least 8 hours or up to 2 days before unmolding.

When ready to use, unwrap and unmold the entire terrine. If it doesn't fall out easily when inverted, wrap a hot towel around it for a minute or two. It should fall right out.

Use as directed in the recipe or serve it on its own with the same garnishes used for the complete terrine.

**NOTES:**

*Sel rose* or pink salt is a curing salt composed of sodium chloride and potassium nitrate that is used for terrines and cured meats. It is available from fine butchers, specialty food stores, or online.

Foie gras is sold in different grades, with Grade A being the premium. Excellent-quality Grade B is generally used to make terrines or pâtés.

# Roasted Quail with Plum Compote

SERVES 6

This is a simple but elegant appetizer. Interestingly, curry powder and other pungent spices were used frequently in recipes of the late nineteenth century, so we feel that using them to accent the gaminess of the quail is reminiscent of Ranhofer's kitchen. The compote can be made a few days in advance and the quail seasoned early in the day and cooked as needed, which makes this a great dish for entertaining.

> 6 semi-boneless quail
>
> 2 tablespoons ground coriander
>
> 2 tablespoons ground fennel
>
> 1 tablespoon curry powder
>
> 2 teaspoons ground cumin
>
> 1 teaspoon freshly ground pepper
>
> Coarse salt to taste
>
> 1 tablespoon corn oil
>
> Plum Compote (recipe follows)
>
> 6 sprigs thyme
>
> 2 tablespoons chopped chives

Rinse the quail under cool running water. Pat dry.

Place the birds on a clean work surface. Using kitchen shears, cut down the seam of each bird's back, open up the bird, and press it flat.

Clip the wings at the first joint, leaving the shoulder bone. French the wing bone—that is, use a small, sharp knife to scrape the meat down and off the bone. Cut each bird in half lengthwise.

Combine the coriander, fennel, curry powder, cumin, and pepper. Set aside.

Preheat the oven to 400°F.

Season the quail with salt and the reserved spice mix. Set aside.

Heat the oil in a large, ovenproof frying pan over medium-high heat. Add the quail, skin side down, and sear, turning once, for 2 minutes, or until colored. Transfer the pan to the preheated oven and roast for about 10 minutes, or until cooked through and golden. Remove from the oven and allow to rest for 3 minutes.

Place about 2 tablespoons of the compote in the center of each of 6 luncheon plates. Crisscross 2 quail halves on top of the compote. Garnish with a sprig of thyme and sprinkle with chopped chives. Serve immediately.

NOTE: Semi-boneless quail is available through specialty markets, butchers, and online.

## Plum Compote

*1 cup sugar*

*Zest and juice of 1 large orange*

*Zest and juice of 1 lemon*

*2 star anise*

*1 cinnamon stick*

*¼ cup plum liqueur or Grand Marnier*

*8 red plums (about 1¾ pounds), washed, dried, and finely diced*

*2 tablespoons finely chopped fresh herbs (such as parsley, chives, tarragon, and thyme, singly or in a combination)*

Combine the sugar with the zest and juice of the orange and the zest of the lemon in a medium heavy-bottom saucepan. Add the star anise and cinnamon stick and stir in the liqueur. Place over medium-low heat and bring to a simmer. Lower the heat and cook at a gentle simmer for about 12 minutes, or until the mixture has become syrupy and thick.

Add the plums along with the lemon juice, stirring to combine. Return the mixture to a simmer and cook, stirring frequently, for about 20 minutes, or until the plums are just tender and the mixture has again become syrupy and thick.

Remove from the heat and set aside. When cool, remove and discard the cinnamon stick. If not using the compote immediately, transfer it to a clean container, cover, and refrigerate until ready to use or for up to 2 weeks.

When ready to serve, fold in the chopped herbs and let come to room temperature.

Of all the recipes collected by the various Delmonico chefs, salads were on the minor list. They were considered to be part of a cold service, not something to be enjoyed alone. A great many of them were in the French tradition of elaborate composed salads, intricately designed with many, many components. Cooked salads were either a mix of vegetables and meats or seafood, or a combination of vegetables. A few were raw vegetable salads—including one using raw eggplant and one with a base of six eight-ounce truffles. Interestingly, there were a number of green salads, which we have found to be served under the *Rôtis* (roast meats or fish) section of large menus along with, generally, roasted game birds.

# Salads

### ROASTED BEET SALAD WITH GOAT CHEESE POPOVERS

### CAESAR SALAD

### ENDIVE, WATERCRESS, AND APPLE SALAD

### WARM ASPARAGUS AND MOREL SALAD WITH MÂCHE AND TRUFFLE VINAIGRETTE

### MONK'S BEARD SALAD WITH BLOOD ORANGE VINAIGRETTE

### GRILLED LOBSTER WITH ARTICHOKES AND HARICOTS VERTS

# Roasted Beet Salad with Goat Cheese Popovers

SERVES 6

On today's menu at Delmonico's, this salad reigns supreme—right after our famous Caesar (see page 96). It has many components, but the complete plate is so beautiful, we urge you to try it. Obviously, you can make as many or as few of them as you wish. Almost everything can be done the day before service, so it is a "Wow!" salad to serve when entertaining.

Use rubber gloves when handling red beets, as they will stain your hands and anything else they come in contact with.

> 2 large red beets (about 3½ inches in diameter), well washed and dried
>
> 3 large yellow beets (about 3½ inches in diameter), well washed and dried
>
> ½ cup olive oil
>
> Coarse salt and freshly ground pepper to taste
>
> Juice of 1 lemon
>
> 2 tablespoons white wine vinegar
>
> 4 cloves garlic, peeled and thinly sliced
>
> 2 shallots, peeled and thinly sliced
>
> 2 cups watercress, tough stems removed
>
> 1 cup tiny frisée leaves
>
> Horseradish Vinaigrette (recipe follows)
>
> Pickled Beets (recipe follows)
>
> Frizzled Beets (recipe follows), optional
>
> Goat Cheese Popovers (recipe follows)
>
> 2 tablespoons chopped chives

Preheat the oven to 325°F.

Place the red and yellow beets on separate large sheets of aluminum foil. Drizzle each beet with 1 tablespoon of olive oil and season with salt and pepper. Fold the foil tightly over the beets. Place the 2 packets on a baking sheet and bake for about 1 hour, or until just tender. Do not overcook or the beets will be too soft. You want a bit of firmness.

While the beets are baking, prepare the marinade.

Combine the light olive oil with the lemon juice and vinegar. Add the garlic and shallots and season with salt and pepper. Set aside.

Remove the beets from the oven and allow them to cool.

Using your fingertips, push the skin from the beets, still keeping the colors separate. Using a mandoline or Japanese vegetable slicer, cut each beet type

From *The Epicurean*: "Dressings or Seasonings for Salads, Tarragon and Chili Vinegar. . . . The quantity of salad to be seasoned and the necessary proportions must be taken into consideration when using these dressings. When a salad is served no oil should ever remain at the bottom of the bowl; the quantity of oil varies with the salad. . . . Americans do not like the taste of oil in which the taste of olive is prominent, and therefore prefer a neutral oil." The reader is also told how to make tarragon vinegar—fill a two-quart jar two thirds with layers of tarragon leaves, shallots, and onions; cover with strong vinegar; and store for two months. A chile pepper variation on the vinegar calls for using hot chiles in place of the tarragon, shallots, and onions. Either one would fit in perfectly in the contemporary kitchen.

crosswise into ⅛-inch-thick slices. You will need 36 slices of each color. Reserve the trimmings to make Pickled Beets.

Using a 2-inch round cookie cutter, carefully cut a circle out of each beet slice. Place each color in a shallow container with a cover. Drizzle the reserved marinade over the beets, cover, and refrigerate for at least 8 hours or overnight.

When ready to serve, combine the watercress and frisée in a medium mixing bowl. Add just enough of the Horseradish Vinaigrette to lightly coat.

Make a semicircle of alternating red and yellow beets slightly in from the edge of each of 6 luncheon plates. Spoon 1 tablespoon of Pickled Beets in the center of each semicircle. Make a mound of the watercress salad on top of the Pickled Beets. Garnish the side with Frizzled Beets, if using, and drizzle a little Horseradish Vinaigrette around the edge of each plate. Place a Goat Cheese Popover on each plate. Sprinkle with chopped chives and serve with the remaining popovers passed on the side.

### HORSERADISH VINAIGRETTE

*2 tablespoons prepared horseradish, drained*

*3 tablespoons white wine vinegar*

*2 tablespoons fresh lemon juice*

*2 teaspoons Dijon mustard*

*1 cup light olive oil*

*Coarse salt and freshly ground pepper to taste*

Combine the horseradish, vinegar, lemon juice, and mustard in a small mixing bowl, whisking to blend well. Slowly whisk in the oil, beating to emulsify. Season with salt and pepper.

Cover and refrigerate until ready to use. Whisk to blend before tossing the salad.

### PICKLED BEETS

*Reserved trimmings from the red and yellow beets in the master recipe,*
*approximately ½ cup from each*

*½ cup cider vinegar*

*2 tablespoons sugar*

Cut the beet trimmings into strips as even as possible. Place in a mixing bowl and set aside.

Combine the vinegar, ¼ cup water, and the sugar in a small, nonreactive saucepan over medium heat. Bring to a boil and simmer for 2 minutes. Pour over the beets.

Cover and refrigerate for 8 hours or overnight.

## FRIZZLED BEETS

*1 large cooked and peeled red beet*

*4 cups vegetable oil*

*Coarse salt and freshly ground pepper to taste*

Using a Japanese vegetable turner (see note), turn the beet into long, thin strands. Place them in a bowl with cold water to cover.

When ready to fry, heat the oil in a deep-fat fryer to 375°F on an instant-read thermometer.

Remove the beet strands from the water and pat as dry as possible.

Working with a few at a time, drop the beet strands into the hot oil and fry for about 30 seconds, or until crisp.

Remove from the oil and place on a double layer of paper towel to drain. Continue frying until all the beets are done.

Season with salt and pepper and serve at room temperature.

NOTE: Japanese vegetable turners make finely cut strips out of vegetables and are available at many kitchen supply marts as well as from Japanese markets.

## GOAT CHEESE POPOVERS

MAKES 12 MINI-POPOVERS

*3 tablespoons salted butter*

*1 cup all-purpose flour, sifted*

*½ teaspoon sugar*

*½ teaspoon salt*

*2 large eggs, at room temperature*

*1 cup milk*

*2 tablespoons melted unsalted butter*

*4 ounces fresh goat cheese, at room temperature*

Preheat the oven to 450°F.

Using the salted butter, generously coat the cups of a 12-cup mini-muffin pan. Set aside.

Combine the flour, sugar, and salt in a blender jar or bowl of a food processor fitted with the metal blade. Add the eggs, milk, and melted butter and process until very smooth.

Fill the mini-muffin cups halfway full. Place a knob of goat cheese in the center of each cup. Pour enough batter into each cup to completely cover the cheese.

Bake for 10 minutes, then reduce the oven temperature to 350°F and continue to bake for an additional 10 minutes, or until the popovers are puffed high and golden brown. Do not open the oven for the first 15 minutes of baking or the popovers will fall. Serve warm.

# Caesar Salad

True, Caesar Salad was not invented at Delmonico's. It hadn't even been created during the heyday of the restaurant, but since we are now a contemporary steak house, it is a must on the menu—every steak house has one. But in honor of our culinary heritage, ours is a bit over-the-top, and it's superb. If you want a simpler salad, you can easily chop some crisp romaine leaves and just toss them with the dressing.

Originally, Caesar salad was prepared tableside by a gloved waiter. This type of service is rarely performed today. We still offer white anchovies on the side to be used at the discretion of the diner.

> *6 cups chopped green romaine lettuce*
>
> *3 cups chopped red romaine lettuce or chopped radicchio*
>
> *Caesar Dressing (recipe follows)*
>
> *18 to 30 small tender romaine leaves*
>
> *Garlic Croutons (recipe follows)*
>
> *Gremolata (recipe follows)*
>
> *6 Asiago Tuiles (recipe follows)*
>
> *12 white anchovy filets*

Place the chopped romaine in a large salad bowl. Add just enough dressing to lightly coat and toss to cover.

Place the romaine leaves in a shallow bowl and drizzle on just enough dressing to lightly coat.

Distribute the leaves among 6 salad plates, arranging them in the center. Mound a good handful of the chopped romaine on top of the leaves. Garnish each plate with croutons and then sprinkle with Gremolata. Nestle an Asiago Tuile in the center and serve with anchovies on the side.

## CAESAR DRESSING

> *1 large farm-fresh egg yolk*
>
> *¼ cup fresh lemon juice*
>
> *3 tablespoons white wine vinegar*
>
> *1½ tablespoons Coleman's dry mustard*
>
> *1 cup canola oil*
>
> *¼ cup freshly grated Parmesan cheese*
>
> *1 tablespoon chopped anchovy filets, well drained*
>
> *1 tablespoon minced capers, well drained*
>
> *Freshly ground white pepper to taste*

Combine the egg yolk, lemon juice, vinegar, and mustard in a medium mixing bowl. Using a handheld immersion blender, process to blend well. With the motor running, slowly add the oil in a steady stream. If the dressing seems too thick, add cool water, a teaspoon at a time, to loosen.

Fold in the cheese, chopped anchovies, and capers until well blended. Season with white pepper.

If not using immediately, cover and refrigerate for up to 6 hours. Re-emulsify before tossing the salad.

## GARLIC CROUTONS

*½ cup olive oil*

*3 cloves garlic, peeled and sliced*

*1 baguette, cut into ½-inch cubes*

*¼ cup chopped flat-leaf parsley*

Combine the oil and garlic in a small saucepan over very low heat. Cook for about 5 minutes, or just until the garlic begins to color. Immediately remove from the heat and allow to cool.

Using a slotted spoon, remove and discard the garlic.

Preheat the oven to 350°F.

Line a baking pan with parchment paper.

Place the bread cubes in a large mixing bowl. Sprinkle with the parsley and then drizzle the garlic-flavored oil over the top, tossing to coat well.

Transfer the seasoned cubes to the prepared baking pan and bake, turning occasionally, for about 5 minutes, or until crisp and golden.

Remove from the oven and allow to cool.

The croutons can be stored airtight in a cool, dark spot for up to 2 days.

## GREMOLATA

*½ cup fresh bread crumbs, toasted*
*3 tablespoons finely minced capers, well drained*
*2 tablespoons freshly grated lemon zest*
*2 tablespoons minced flat-leaf parsley*
*Coarse salt and freshly cracked black pepper to taste*

Combine all the ingredients in a small mixing bowl. Cover and set aside until ready to use.

## ASIAGO TUILES

*½ cup freshly grated Asiago cheese*

Preheat the oven to 325°F.

Line a baking pan with a nonstick silicone liner.

Place a 2-inch round cookie cutter on the liner and sprinkle an even layer of cheese (about 1 tablespoon) inside the circle. Continue making cheese circles, leaving about 2 inches between each one, until you have made eight. (You will only need six, but you may have some breakage.)

Bake the tuiles for about 4 minutes, or until the cheese circles have melted into 2-inch solid disks.

Remove from the oven and set aside to cool.

Carefully remove the disks from the pan, keeping them whole. They can be stored, separated by waxed paper, airtight, for up to a day.

# Endive, Watercress, and Apple Salad

SERVES 6

This is a tribute to Charles Ranhofer, who introduced endive to New York diners. He also loved to incorporate apples into dishes and always had watercress as a garnish. It is a simple salad with a light, refreshing vinaigrette.

*3 tablespoons fresh lemon juice*

*3 tablespoons fresh lime juice*

*2 tablespoons white wine vinegar*

*2 tablespoons honey*

*2 teaspoons Dijon mustard*

*1 cup extra-virgin olive oil*

*Coarse salt and freshly ground pepper to taste*

*3 endives, washed, trimmed, and cut into julienne*

*1 red apple, washed, cored, and cut into julienne*

*1 green apple, washed, cored, and cut into julienne*

*1½ cups watercress, tough stems removed*

*1 tablespoon lemon thyme leaves, optional garnish*

Combine the lemon and lime juices with the vinegar, honey, and mustard in a small mixing bowl. Add the oil in a slow, steady stream, whisking constantly until well emulsified. Season with salt and pepper. Set aside.

Combine the endive, red and green apple, and watercress in a salad bowl. Add just enough vinaigrette to moisten, tossing to coat.

Distribute the salad onto 6 salad plates. Drizzle a bit more vinaigrette around the edge of each plate. Sprinkle the plates with lemon thyme leaves, if using, and serve.

NOTE: This a wonderful base salad for any protein but works particularly well with a chicken paillard, which is a boneless, skinned breast that has been pounded flat. Marinate the chicken breast in lemon juice, garlic, thyme, rosemary, and extra-virgin olive oil for an hour and then cook quickly on a grill.

# Warm Asparagus and Morel Salad with Mâche and Truffle Vinaigrette

SERVES 6

This is a perfect spring salad—one very reminiscent of more lavish eras. Mâche, also known as lamb's lettuce (because it grows wild in corn fields or, perhaps, because its leaves are as soft as lamb's wool) comes in tiny bunches that are very sweet and add beauty to the plate. If you have any left over, the vinaigrette is great to keep on hand for use as a sauce for rich, white fish such as halibut or for grilled meats.

> ½ pound slab bacon, cut into small cubes
>
> 6 ounces fresh morels, well cleaned
>
> 18 stalks white asparagus, tough ends removed,
>    cut into 1-inch pieces on the bias, and blanched
>
> 18 stalks green asparagus, tough ends removed,
>    cut into 1-inch pieces on the bias, and blanched
>
> Black Truffle Vinaigrette (recipe follows)
>
> Coarse salt and freshly ground pepper to taste
>
> 12 small bunches mâche, carefully washed and dried
>
> 3 tablespoons chopped chives

Place the bacon in a frying pan over medium-low heat. Fry, stirring occasionally, for about 12 minutes, or until all the fat has been rendered and the bacon is crisp and golden. Using a slotted spoon, transfer the bacon to a double layer of paper towel to drain.

Keeping the pan on the heat, add the morels and sauté for about 2 minutes, or until just beginning to brown around the edges. Add the asparagus and sauté for about 3 minutes, or until the pieces are warmed through.

Remove the pan from the heat and add the reserved bacon, tossing to combine. Add about ¼ cup of the vinaigrette and again toss to combine. Taste and season with salt and pepper.

Place the mâche in a mixing bowl. Add just a bit of the vinaigrette to barely moisten. Set aside.

Distribute the asparagus mixture among 6 salad plates. Place 2 small mounds of mâche on top of the asparagus on each plate. Drizzle a bit of vinaigrette around each plate, sprinkle with chopped chives, and serve.

## BLACK TRUFFLE VINAIGRETTE

*2 cups port wine*

*1 teaspoon unsalted butter*

*¼ cup chopped black truffles*

*2 tablespoons minced shallots*

*2 tablespoons white wine vinegar*

*¾ cup olive oil*

*¼ cup white truffle oil (see page 119)*

*Coarse salt and freshly ground pepper to taste*

Place the port in a small nonreactive saucepan over medium heat. Bring to a boil. Lower the heat and simmer for about 30 minutes, or until reduced to ¼ cup. Remove from the heat and allow to cool.

Heat the butter in a small sauté pan over medium heat. Add the chopped truffles and shallots and sauté for about 1 minute, or just until the shallots have softened slightly.

Remove from the heat and allow to cool.

Transfer the reduced port to a small mixing bowl. Add the truffle mixture, along with the vinegar.

Combine the olive oil and truffle oil and, whisking constantly, add the oils to the port mixture, beating until well emulsified. Season with salt and pepper.

If not using immediately, cover and set aside for up to 4 hours. For longer storage, cover and refrigerate. Bring the dressing to room temperature and re-emulsify before tossing the salad.

# Monk's Beard Salad with Blood Orange Vinaigrette

SERVES 6

To quote *The Epicurean*, "this salad is very much loved and is exceedingly wholesome." Monk's beard is a type of chicory very rarely seen in America (see note). Apparently it was such a tasty green that all that was required to serve it was a bit of oil, vinegar, and salt and pepper—a few slices of beetroot were often added for color. We have substituted the more readily available frisée. You could also use purslane, dandelion, or other small, flavorful greens that would pair well with a sweet vinaigrette to soften the bitterness.

> *2 cups fresh blood orange juice*
>
> *1 tablespoon sugar*
>
> *4 sprigs mint, plus additional mint leaves to make 1 tablespoon chiffonade*
>
> *¼ cup champagne vinegar*
>
> *1 cup olive oil*
>
> *Coarse salt and freshly ground pepper to taste*
>
> *6 clementines, peeled and cut into suprêmes*
>
> *6 small heads frisée, preferably with mostly white leaves*
>
> *Cracked black pepper to taste*

Place the orange juice and sugar in a small nonreactive saucepan over medium heat. Add the 4 mint sprigs and bring to a simmer. Cook gently for about 20 minutes, or until reduced to ½ cup. Remove from the heat and set aside to cool.

Remove the mint sprigs from the reduced juice. Add the vinegar and, using a handheld immersion blender, pulse to blend. Add the oil and pulse to emulsify. Season with salt and pepper. Fold in the clementines. Set aside.

Leaving the frisée heads intact, wash them well and pat very dry. Trim off any brown parts. Carefully cut out the core from the bottom, holding the head together. Carefully transfer the complete head, top facing up, to an individual salad plate.

Fold the tablespoon of mint chiffonade into the vinaigrette. Spoon the vinaigrette over the frisée on each plate, making sure that each plate has a few suprêmes. Grind some cracked black pepper over the top and serve.

NOTE: Monk's beard is a slightly bitter green that is native to Tuscany, where it was originally cultivated by Capuchin monks, hence its name. It is available for only a very short period each year. We have seen it on English (where it is known as "goat's beard" or "Johnny go to bed at noon") and European menus. It may make its way back into American menus as the expansion of heritage vegetables and farmers markets increases.

# Grilled Lobster with Artichokes and Haricots Verts

SERVES 6

This simple, elegant lobster dish is great for summer entertaining, as much of the preparation can be done in advance. The vanilla vinaigrette adds a note of sweet acidity that is a wonderful match to the rich lobster.

*Three 1¼-pound live lobsters*

*12 cooked artichoke hearts, halved*

*½ pound haricots verts, trimmed, blanched, and cut, on the bias, into 1-inch pieces*

*½ pound cooked fingerling potatoes, cut into pieces on the bias*

*Vanilla Vinaigrette (recipe follows)*

*Coarse salt and freshly ground pepper to taste*

*3 cups mesclun or other small salad greens, well washed and dried*

*1½ tablespoons chopped mixed fresh herbs, such as tarragon, oregano, and parsley*

Place a lobster on a cutting board. Using a sharp chef's knife held vertically, plunge the point into the lobster's head about 1 inch behind the eyes. Push the knife completely in to touch the cutting board and then move it forward to cut the entire head in half. This is the quickest and easiest method of killing a live lobster. Pull the claws from the body. Repeat with the remaining two lobsters.

Prepare an ice water bath in a large bowl and set it aside.

Place the claws and bodies in the top half of a steamer over boiling water. Cover and steam them for 4 minutes. Remove the bodies and continue steaming the claws for an additional 3 minutes. Immerse both the bodies and claws in the ice water bath as soon as they are removed from the steamer to stop the cooking.

Crack the shells on the bodies and claws and carefully remove the meat, keeping it in pieces as large as possible. It is particularly nice to have a whole claw for garnish.

Combine the artichoke hearts, haricots verts, and potatoes in a mixing bowl. Add about ½ cup of the vinaigrette, tossing to coat well. Season with salt and pepper. Set aside.

Preheat and oil the grill.

Using a pastry brush, generously coat the lobster meat with the vinaigrette. Season it with salt and pepper and grill, turning it frequently, for about 3 minutes, or just until nicely marked. Using tongs, carefully remove the lobster from the grill.

Add the salad greens to the marinating vegetables, tossing to coat.

Place equal portions of the salad in the center of each of 6 luncheon plates, mounding slightly. Distribute the lobster meat among the salads, laying a whole claw over the top, of possible. Sprinkle the top with chopped herbs and serve.

## VANILLA VINAIGRETTE

*1 cup canola oil*

*½ vanilla bean*

*1 teaspoon unsalted butter*

*2 tablespoons minced shallots*

*½ teaspoon minced garlic*

*1 large farm-fresh egg yolk*

*2 tablespoons Champagne vinegar*

*6 tablespoons fresh orange juice*

*3 tablespoons fresh lime juice*

*Coarse salt and freshly ground pepper to taste*

*2 teaspoons chopped fresh tarragon*

Place the oil in a small heavy saucepan over low heat. Using a small, sharp knife, split the vanilla bean in half lengthwise and scrape the seeds into the oil. Add the split bean, bring to a bare simmer, and cook gently for 5 minutes. Turn off the heat and allow the oil to infuse for 1 hour.

Remove and discard the vanilla bean from the oil. Set the oil aside.

Heat the butter in a small sauté pan over medium-low heat. Add the shallots and garlic and sauté for about 2 minutes, or just until the vegetables have softened. Remove from the heat and set aside to cool.

Combine the egg yolk with the cooled shallots and garlic in a small bowl. Add the vinegar, along with the orange and lime juices. Using a handheld immersion blender, pulse to combine. Add about ¾ cup of the reserved vanilla oil and pulse to emulsify, adding more oil if needed. Season with salt and pepper.

When ready to serve, stir in the tarragon.

On the early Delmonico's menus, side dishes as we now know them were referred to as *Entremets de Legumes*. The French *entremets* means "in-between dishes" and is derived from the term describing the minstrel entertainment offered between courses of a banquet during the Middle Ages. If used at all today, the term generally is applied to desserts.

In both of the extensive cookbooks written by Ranhofer and Filippini, the vegetable dishes were often elaborately sauced and complicated to make. Many dishes, such as timbales and purées, which we would now consider side dishes, were regarded as garnishes to decorate elaborately plated roasts. In this section, we have offered a combination of all of these as we now feature them on the menu.

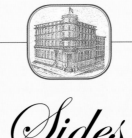

# Sides

EGGPLANT TIMBALE

GLAZED ENDIVE

CREAMED SPINACH

ROOT VEGETABLE POT PIE

THE DELMONICO POTATO

HERBED HASH BROWN POTATOES

DELMONICO'S ORIGINAL MACARONI
WITH CREAM AND TRUFFLES

BUTTERNUT SQUASH RISOTTO

# Eggplant Timbale

SERVES 6

Eggplant was a vegetable that was not much known in America when it was first featured on the Delmonico's menu. Timbales, however, were prepared in many guises, always in classic timbale molds and beautifully decorated. Here we use eggplant in a contemporary timbale simply made in a metal ring mold.

½ cup olive oil

2 cloves garlic, peeled and smashed

6 roasted red bell peppers, cut in half, stemmed, and seeded

2 long, thin yellow zucchini

1 long, thin green zucchini

12 shiitake mushroom caps, at least 2 inches in diameter

1 long, thin Japanese eggplant, well washed, trimmed,
    and cut crosswise into ⅛-inch-thick slices

2 tablespoons red wine vinegar

2 tablespoons fresh thyme leaves

2 tablespoons chopped flat-leaf parsley

Coarse salt and freshly ground black pepper to taste

12 heaping tablespoons (6 ounces) Boursin cheese, at room temperature

Preheat the oven to 400°F.

Combine the oil and garlic in a small saucepan over medium heat. Bring to a simmer. Immediately remove from the heat and set aside to steep for 1 hour. Remove and discard the garlic.

Using a 2½-inch round cutter, cut the red bell pepper into 2½-inch circles. Place the circles in a large mixing bowl.

Trim the yellow and green zucchini and then cut each one, crosswise on the bias, into ⅛-inch-thick slices. Add to the peppers.

Using a small, sharp knife, lightly score the shiitake caps on the diagonal. Add the mushrooms along with the eggplant to the other vegetables.

Add the reserved garlic-flavored oil, vinegar, thyme, parsley, and salt and pepper to taste. Set aside for 30 minutes.

Lightly coat 2 nonstick baking pans with nonstick vegetable spray. Lay the eggplant, green and yellow zucchini, and mushrooms out in a single layer in the pans. Place in the preheated oven and roast, checking frequently, as some of the vegetables will cook quicker than others, for about 12 minutes, or until nicely colored.

Remove from the oven and set aside to cool.

If using immediately, lower the oven temperature to 375°F.

Place a 2½-inch round ring mold on a baking sheet lined with parchment paper and begin making vegetable layers, starting with the eggplant, followed by 2 slices green zucchini, 2 slices yellow zucchini, then a bell pepper round. Top the pepper with a heaping tablespoon of the cheese, patting it down to make a smooth, even layer. Place a mushroom cap on top. Repeat the layering one more time, ending with a mushroom cap. You can now slide the ring mold up and off the timbale and use it again, but if you have 6 ring molds, it is easier to make all of the timbales at once.

If serving immediately, bake the finished timbales for about 10 minutes to soften the cheese and heat through the layers.

If not using immediately, cover with plastic film and refrigerate for up to 3 days. Reheat as above just before serving, allowing a bit more time if the timbales are chilled when they go into the oven.

OPPOSITE: Illustrations from *The Epicurean* of various styles of timbales

BELOW (CLOCKWISE FROM TOP): Eggplant Timbale, Glazed Endive, and Creamed Spinach

# Glazed Endive

Endive was just one of the many ingredients that Charles Ranhofer introduced to Delmonico diners. It was not easily obtained and was therefore considered a great delicacy. There is only one recipe for endive in *The Epicurean*, and it is entitled *Endives ou Escaroles Glacées*, glazed endive or escarole. We tried making the dish as directed—simply braising endive in a buttered pan—but found it to be much too bitter. We think that the original was probably made with what would be to contemporary diners an excessive amount of butter, at least 1 cup. Instead we devised this somewhat more elaborate preparation, which results in a meltingly soft and sweet dish.

> 3 tablespoons unsalted butter
> 3 Belgian endives, trimmed and cut in half, lengthwise
> ¼ cup brandy
> ¼ cup ruby red grapefruit juice
> 1 tablespoon sugar
> Coarse salt and freshly ground pepper to taste

Heat 2 tablespoons of the butter in a medium sauté pan over medium-low heat. Add the endives, cut sides down. Allow to cook for about 7 minutes, or until softened and lightly colored.

Turn the endives, cover, and cook, watching carefully to prevent burning, for about another 7 minutes, or until lightly colored.

Add the brandy. Turn the pan slightly so that the flame of the stove will ignite the alcohol in the brandy, or carefully use a match. Lift the pan from the heat and let the fire die down. Return the pan to the heat and simmer for about 2 minutes, or until reduced by half. Add the grapefruit juice and sprinkle the sugar over the top. Season with salt and pepper and simmer for 2 minutes. Add the remaining 1 tablespoon butter and swirl the pan to incorporate it and thicken the sauce slightly.

Remove from the heat and serve.

# Creamed Spinach

SERVES 6

We couldn't survive in the steak house tradition without creamed spinach on the menu. Fortunately, this dish has been served at Delmonico's throughout its history, so we didn't have to look far for the perfect recipe. Early versions called for a bit of flour to be added with the cream, but we use Parmesan cheese as the thickener for a rich and satisfying side dish.

You can also serve the spinach in individual ramekins or place it in a baking dish, sprinkle the top with grated Parmesan, and broil for a few minutes to glaze the surface.

> *3 cups well-drained, squeezed-dry chopped spinach*
> *3 cups Parmesan Cream (recipe follows)*
> *Coarse salt and freshly ground pepper to taste*

Combine the spinach and Parmesan Cream in a heavy saucepan over medium heat. Season with salt and pepper, beating to incorporate the cream into the spinach. Bring to a simmer and cook for about 5 minutes, or until the cream has been absorbed by the spinach and the mixture has thickened slightly.

Remove the saucepan from the heat and, using a handheld immersion blender, pulse to smooth slightly.

Serve hot in a covered serving dish.

### PARMESAN CREAM

> *2 tablespoons unsalted butter*
> *2 shallots, peeled and minced*
> *1 clove garlic, peeled and minced*
> *¼ cup dry white wine*
> *2 tablespoons all-purpose flour*
> *4 cups heavy cream*
> *Pinch ground nutmeg*
> *½ cup grated Parmesan cheese*

Heat the butter in a large saucepan over medium heat. Add the shallots and garlic and cook, stirring occasionally, for about 3 minutes, or until translucent. Add the wine and cook for about 3 minutes, or until slightly reduced. Add the flour and stir until smooth. Beat in the cream and nutmeg and bring to a boil, watching carefully so that the liquid doesn't boil over the pan. Lower the heat and simmer for about 10 minutes, or until the cream begins to thicken.

Remove from the heat and whisk in the cheese.

If not using immediately, transfer to a clean container, cover, and refrigerate for up to 3 days.

The classic Delmonico's *Épinards à la Crème* was achieved by using only the youngest, tenderest spinach leaves. The cooks washed them in 5 or 6 turns of cold water and then quickly blanched them in boiling, salted water. They drained the leaves and then pressed and pressed and pressed to remove any remnant of moisture. After finely chopping the spinach, they cooked it over a very hot fire with lots of butter, stirring vigorously until all the moisture was gone. The mixture was sprinkled with flour and seasoned with salt and pepper, and then enough cream to moisten was beaten in. Just before serving, more butter was incorporated and the dish was garnished with puff paste crescents or small *bouchées* filled with béchamel sauce.

# Root Vegetable Pot Pie

MAKES 6

This is another take on the Victorian timbale. We serve it with our roast chicken (see page 150) in the restaurant, but it works with almost any meat or poultry. Since the pot pies can be made in advance and baked just before serving, they are an elegant (and easy) dish for dinner parties.

You need six three-inch round ring molds to make individual pot pies. If you don't have them, you could also use the outer ring of a small springform pan to make one large pie, which could then be cut into wedges when serving.

*½ cup dry white wine*

*6 tablespoons unsalted butter*

*Coarse salt and freshly ground pepper to taste*

*1 pound rutabaga, peeled and diced*

*1 tablespoon light brown sugar*

*Juice of 1 lemon*

*1 celery root (about 12 ounces)*

*1¾ cups mashed potatoes*

*1 large egg*

*Caramelized Onions (recipe follows)*

*¾ cup chopped cooked wild mushrooms (see note)*

Combine the wine and 2 tablespoons of the butter with 2 cups cold water in a medium saucepan over medium heat. Bring to a boil, season with salt and pepper, and lower the heat. Simmer for 3 minutes. Remove from the heat and set aside to cool.

Place the rutabaga in a medium saucepan with cold, salted water to cover by 1 inch. Bring to a boil over high heat. Lower the heat and simmer for about 12 minutes, or until very tender.

Remove from the heat, drain well, and allow to cool. Then roughly mash with a table fork. Season with salt, pepper, and brown sugar and set aside.

Pour the lemon juice into a bowl of cold water. Set aside.

Peel and trim the celery root. Using a mandoline or Japanese vegetable slicer, cut the root, crosswise, into twelve ⅛-inch-thick slices. As you slice, place the root in the acidulated water to keep it from discoloring.

Preheat the oven to 375°F. Line a baking sheet with parchment paper.

Using 2 tablespoons of the butter, generously coat the interior of six 3-inch ring molds. Place the buttered ring molds directly on the parchment-lined baking sheet.

Combine the mashed potatoes with the egg and beat with a wooden spoon to incorporate well. Season with salt and pepper. Transfer the potatoes to a pastry bag fitted with a scalloped tip. Set aside.

Divide the mashed rutabaga into 6 equal portions.

Pat a celery root round dry and place it in the bottom of a 3-inch ring mold. Pack a portion of the rutabaga on top of the celery root, smoothing it to an even layer. Top with an even layer of Caramelized Onions. Top the onions with a layer of mushrooms, making a smooth, even layer. Pipe about ¼ cup of the potatoes on top in an attractive scallop design.

When all the pot pies have been made, melt the remaining 2 tablespoons butter and, using a pastry brush, lightly coat the tops with it. Bake the pot pies for about 10 minutes, or until the celery root is tender and the center is very hot.

Remove from the oven, lift off the ring molds, and serve.

NOTE: You will need approximately ¼-pound of raw mushrooms to yield ¾ cup chopped, cooked mushrooms. The raw mushrooms should be sliced, sautéed in 2 tablespoons of butter or olive oil, seasoned with salt and pepper to taste, and chopped.

## CARAMELIZED ONIONS

*2 tablespoons olive oil*
*2 tablespoons unsalted butter*
*2 large onions, peeled and finely sliced*
*2 teaspoons light brown sugar*
*Coarse salt and freshly ground pepper to taste*

Heat the oil and butter in a large sauté pan over medium heat. Add the onions and sprinkle with the sugar. Cook, stirring occasionally, for 12 to 15 minutes, or until the onions are deeply colored and very soft. Season with salt and pepper. Remove from the heat and set aside to cool. Use immediately or store, covered and refrigerated, for up to 1 week.

## The Delmonico Potato

Although Delmonico potatoes have appeared on menus worldwide, there doesn't seem to be a definitive recipe. Alessandro Filippini offered a recipe for them in his seminal cookbook of the nineteenth century, *The International Cook Book*, but even so every hotel and restaurant seemed to create its own version. In *The Epicurean*, Charles Ranhofer does not even mention them. However, no matter the inventor, Delmonico potatoes are always bursting with cream and butter, and we think our current version hits that mark.

> 6 very large Idaho potatoes, well washed and dried
> Oil for coating potatoes
> ½ cup (1 stick) melted unsalted butter
> Potato Gratin (recipe follows)

Preheat the oven to 375°F.

Pierce the potatoes with a table fork. Lightly coat with the oil and bake for about 1 hour, or until the tip of a small, sharp knife is easily inserted into the center.

Remove from the oven and set aside until cool enough to handle.

Turn the oven temperature to broil.

Place the cooled potatoes on a cutting board. Using a small, sharp knife, carefully cut out the top of each potato, leaving about a ¼-inch border all around. Scoop the flesh out of each potato, leaving a neat shell. Reserve the flesh to make mashed potatoes, potato soup, or a gratin on another day.

Using a pastry brush, generously coat each shell, inside and out, with melted butter. Place the buttered shells on a broiler pan and broil, watching carefully, for about 6 minutes, or until crisp.

Remove from the broiler.

Return the oven temperature to 400°F.

Divide the gratin into 6 equal portions. Pack a portion into each potato shell, mounding to overstuff it. (The potatoes can be made up to this point and stored, covered and refrigerated, for up to 2 days.)

Using a pastry brush, lightly coat the top of each potato with melted butter. Bake for 10 minutes, or until the interior is hot and the top is crusty. (If the potatoes have been refrigerated, they will require substantially more baking—up to 30 minutes.)

Serve piping hot.

---

### Delmonico Potatoes

"Place four good-sized boiled and finely handshed potatoes in a frying pan with one and a half gills cold milk, half gill cream, two saltspoons salt, one saltspoon white pepper, and a saltspoon grated nutmeg; mix well and cook on the range for ten minutes, lightly mixing occasionally. Then add one tablespoon grated Parmesan cheese, lightly mix again. Transfer the potatoes into a gratin dish, sprinkle another light tablespoon grated Parmesan cheese over and set in the oven to bake for six minutes, or until they have obtained a good golden colour, remove and serve."

From *The International Cook Book* by Alessandro Filippini

## POTATO GRATIN

*1 cup milk*

*1 cup heavy cream*

*2 cups finely sliced leeks, white part only*

*1 tablespoon roasted garlic purée (see note)*

*1 tablespoon chopped rosemary leaves*

*Pinch freshly ground nutmeg*

*Coarse salt and freshly ground white pepper to taste*

*5 tablespoons unsalted butter, at room temperature*

*4 large Yukon Gold potatoes, peeled and cut, crosswise, into ⅛-inch-thick slices*

Preheat the oven to 400°F.

Combine the milk and cream with the leeks, garlic purée, rosemary, and nutmeg in a large heavy saucepan over medium heat. Add salt and white pepper and bring to a simmer. Whisk in 3 tablespoons of the butter, remove from the pan from the heat, and keep warm.

Using the remaining butter, generously coat the interior of an 11-by-7-by-2-inch baking pan. Set aside.

Season the potatoes with salt and pepper. Using about half of the potatoes, cover the bottom of the prepared pan with a layer of slightly overlapping potato slices. Pour half of the milk mixture over the potatoes. Make another layer with the remaining potatoes and cover it with the remaining milk mixture.

Bake for about 1 hour, or until the tip of a small, sharp knife is easily inserted into the center.

Remove from the heat and use as directed in the above recipe or as a side dish with meat, game, or poultry.

NOTE: To make roasted garlic purée, take a head of garlic and slice off the top, then wrap the entire head in aluminum foil. Place the packet in a 350°F oven and roast for 30 minutes, or until the garlic cloves are soft. Gently squeeze out enough purée, as required. The roasted garlic keeps well refrigerated.

# Herbed Hash Brown Potatoes

Every contemporary steak house has a hash brown potato dish on the menu, but we think that the one we have devised is absolutely the best version you will ever taste: Crisp on the outside and sweet and buttery soft in the interior. The perfect accompaniment to a juicy steak.

> 3½ pounds Yukon gold potatoes, peeled and cut into small dice
>
> 3 tablespoons unsalted butter, at room temperature
>
> Coarse salt and freshly ground pepper to taste
>
> 6 tablespoons clarified butter
>
> 1 tablespoon roasted garlic purée
>
> 1 teaspoon lemon thyme leaves
>
> 2½ tablespoons Caramelized Onions (see page 113)

Place the potatoes in a large sauté pan. Add 2½ cups water along with the butter and salt and pepper. Place over high heat, then lower flame when it simmers and cook, stirring occasionally, as you would for risotto, until all the water has been absorbed. Add another cup of water and continue to cook, stirring occasionally, for about 15 minutes, or until the potatoes are tender and all the water has again been absorbed.

Remove from the heat and set aside.

Preheat the oven to 500°F.

Place ¼ cup of the clarified butter in a 10½-inch ovenproof skillet with rounded sides over medium-high heat. Add the potatoes and cook, stirring occasionally, for about 2 minutes, or just until the potatoes begin to color. Stir in the roasted garlic and thyme and season with salt and pepper. Continue to cook, tossing frequently, for about 7 minutes, or until the potatoes are evenly browned.

Remove from the heat and scrape the potatoes onto a plate. Set aside.

Using a paper towel, wipe the skillet clean.

Return the skillet to medium-high heat. Add the remaining 2 tablespoons of clarified butter. Pack half of the reserved potatoes into the bottom of the skillet. Place the onions on top and, using a spatula, spread them out to an even layer. Top with the remaining potatoes, flattening them down into the pan to make a tight fit. You want the finished dish to be smooth and even on all sides.

Bake for 15 minutes, or until golden brown on top and heated through.

Remove the potatoes from the oven and place a 12-inch plate over the top. Invert the skillet, allowing the potato cake to drop onto the plate.

Serve immediately, cut into wedges.

# Delmonico's Original Macaroni with Cream and Truffles

SERVES 6

Like almost every other dish on the early Delmonico's menus, plain old mac 'n' cheese got gussied up with truffles. We've taken it even higher with a combination of cheeses—early recipes used Cheddar—the addition of truffle oil, and the use of more interesting pasta shapes. You can, of course, go back to the original—Cheddar and white truffles—if you're a purist.

*½ cup (1 stick) unsalted butter*

*1 cup shredded Fontina cheese*

*1 cup shredded Gruyère cheese*

*1 cup shredded Taleggio cheese*

*1 medium onion, peeled and minced*

*¼ cup sifted all-purpose flour*

*2 cups hot milk*

*Pinch freshly grated nutmeg*

*1 pound dried cavatappi, orecchiette, small shell,*
*    or elbow pasta, cooked as directed on package and drained*

*¼ cup chopped chives, tarragon, or flat-leaf parsley*

*Coarse salt and freshly ground pepper to taste*

*½ cup freshly grated Parmesan cheese*

*⅓ cup fresh bread crumbs*

*2 tablespoons white truffle oil (see note)*

*4 ounces black truffle (see note)*

Preheat the oven to 350°F.

Using 2 tablespoons of the butter, generously coat the interior of a 4-quart shallow baking dish or casserole. Set aside.

Combine the Fontina, Gruyère, and Taleggio in a mixing bowl. Set aside.

Heat ¼ cup of the butter in a large saucepan over medium heat. Add the onion and cook, stirring frequently, for about 3 minutes, or until soft. Stirring constantly, add the flour and continue to cook for another 3 minutes. Continue stirring as you add the milk.

Add the nutmeg and cook, stirring frequently, until the mixture comes to a simmer. Adjust the heat and simmer for 3 minutes.

Remove the milk mixture from the heat and add the reserved cheeses, a bit at a time, beating constantly to melt the cheese into the milk.

When all of the cheese has been added, stir in the reserved pasta. Add the herbs and season with salt and pepper.

Transfer the pasta mixture into the prepared baking dish, smoothing out slightly. Sprinkle the top with Parmesan cheese, followed by the bread crumbs. Dot the top with bits of the remaining 2 tablespoons butter.

Bake for 25 minutes, or until bubbling.

Increase the oven temperature to broil and broil for about 2 minutes, or until the top is golden brown and crunchy.

Remove from the broiler. Drizzle the top with truffle oil and, at the table, shave the truffle over the top. When scooping out individual servings, shave a few more truffle pieces over each one. Serve piping hot.

NOTE: White truffle oil and black truffles are available from most specialty food stores or online (see Sources).

# Butternut Squash Risotto

SERVES 6

Throughout the cookbooks by the early Delmonico's chefs we saw references to "risot," which surprised us. Digging further, we found gnocchi and many styles of macaroni as well. We had thought that rice timbales and egg noodles would be about the only fancy starches served at this time in American culinary history. It turns out that risotti, ravioli, and other pastas are not so contemporary after all.

To make this recipe exactly, you will need an electric juicer. However, the juice can be replaced with chicken stock, but the flavor and color will be quite different.

*3 butternut squash*

*5 tablespoons melted unsalted butter*

*1 tablespoon olive oil*

*Coarse salt and freshly ground pepper to taste*

*3 cups vegetable broth or water, plus more, if needed*

*¾ cup finely chopped Spanish onion*

*1½ cups Arborio rice*

*1 cup dry white wine*

*¼ cup grated Parmesan cheese*

*1 tablespoon chopped sage*

*1 tablespoon chopped flat-leaf parsley*

Using a sharp knife, cut the neck off of each squash. You will only be using the necks for this recipe. Reserve the bottoms for another use, such as bowls for soup.

Peel and cut 1 of the squash necks into a very small dice. Place the diced squash in a steamer basket over simmering water, cover, and steam for about 4 minutes, or until the squash is just barely tender. Transfer the squash to a mixing bowl. Melt 1 tablespoon of the butter and add it, along with the olive oil, salt, and pepper, to the mixing bowl, tossing to coat well. Set aside.

While the squash is steaming, peel and chop the remaining 2 squash necks. Place the pieces in a juicer and process to make 2 cups of squash juice. If this does not yield 2 cups, you will have to make up the difference with broth or water.

Combine the squash juice with the vegetable broth in a medium saucepan over medium heat. Bring to a simmer, then lower the heat and keep the liquid very hot.

Heat 2 tablespoons of the butter in a large nonstick pan (or risotto pan) over medium heat. Add the onion and sauté for about 3 minutes, or just until the onion is soft. Add the rice and stir for about 2 minutes, or until the rice is well coated with butter and glistening.

Add the wine and cook, stirring the rice in one direction only, for about 5 minutes, or until the pan is almost dry.

Begin ladling in the hot broth mixture, ½ cup at a time, continuing to stir the rice in one direction only and shaking the pan from time to time. Add each additional ½ cup only after the previous addition has been absorbed by the rice. It should take about 20 minutes for the rice to absorb all of the broth mixture and turn creamy with some resistance when chewed.

Remove the risotto from the heat and stir in the remaining 2 tablespoons of butter. Fold in the reserved steamed squash. Season with salt and white pepper. Fold in the cheese, chopped sage and parsley, and serve.

NOTE: If you would like to serve the risotto as an entrée, cut the necks from 6 squash and hollow out the bottoms, leaving about a ¼-inch edge to form a bowl. Season the interior of the "bowls" with melted butter, salt, and pepper and bake them for about 20 minutes in a preheated 350°F oven, or until just about tender but still firm.

Although Delmonico's early fame was based on its execution of the classic French culinary repertoire (with the introduction of American ingenuity and ingredients), the restaurant is now known as a classic American steak house. Beef was often the center of the table in the early days of the restaurant also, but a much wider variety of meat and game was featured than is found on our current menu.

# Meat and Game

DELMONICO STEAK

TENDERLOIN OF BEEF WITH
SWEET POTATO CROQUETTES

TENDERLOIN HASH

VEAL SWEETBREADS WITH MORELS AND
FAVA BEANS AND GOLDEN RAISIN PURÉE

HERB-ROASTED RACK OF LAMB

PORK CUTLETS WITH APPLE FRITTERS

CROWN ROAST OF PORK WITH
SAUSAGE STUFFING

VENISON MEDALLIONS WITH
GINGER CRANBERRY SAUCE

We now emphasize American beef but do feature other superb meats and, occasionally, game.

It has been very interesting for us to research the types of meat served in the restaurant during its heyday. One of the most impressive cuts of beef that proclaimed excess was a baron. This was the saddle of beef, weighing about 150 pounds, cut from the hip of a young steer as far down as the second rib. The thinner section was covered in fat to make the entire piece of an equal size so that it would cook uniformly. It was generally roasted in the bakery's brick oven and served with slivers of fresh horseradish, Yorkshire pudding, and roasted potatoes.

Although we no longer roast or eat such huge portions, recent years have brought an enormous demand for large, juicy prime beef steaks. This demand, coupled with the fact that not much prime beef comes to market, has made it extremely difficult to find. We at Delmonico's have had to become experts at finding and handling the high-quality beef that is served in the restaurant. Dennis Turcinovic, our young, dynamic managing partner, has the difficult job of searching out the very best for us.

The highest-grade prime beef is extensively marbled with cream-colored fat, which produces a juicy, succulent steak with a great depth of flavor. Only about 2 percent of the beef that comes to market is so labeled, and it is a test of Dennis's skill that it frequents the Delmonico's table.

The best beef is brilliant red, very tightly grained, and well marbled with fat. It usually comes from an animal between eighteen months and two years of age. In America cattle are generally hay- or grass-fed only during the early stages of growth and then fattened on a high-energy diet of rich grains. For the most part, animals from other parts of the world are completely grass-fed, which results in a tougher, gamier, leaner meat. With increasing concerns about environment and health, farmers are returning to older methods of breeding and raising cattle, and heritage breeds are being reintroduced into the market.

Dennis continually works with our meat purveyors to ensure that all the meat served in the restaurant is the

market's best. He also searches for small farmers who can provide special cuts and prime examples of the butcher's art. Although we continue to offer a variety of grilled, roasted, and braised meats, it is steak that reigns supreme. As we often say, where else would you eat a Delmonico steak but at Delmonico's?

# Delmonico Steak

SERVES 6

This is, to us at Delmonico's, the one and only Delmonico Steak. We use a boneless, twenty-ounce, prime rib-eye steak that has been aged for at least six weeks. Extremely tender yet unbelievably flavorful, this steak is cut from the center of the rib section. To finish it, we top the sizzling steak with a bit of what we call "Meat Butter," a herbaceous compound butter mix that is easy to make and simple to keep on hand.

Because fires vary in degree of heat, it is difficult to estimate the length of time it will take a steak to cook. Since restaurant stoves are so much hotter than those in most homes, we have given instructions for grilling on a gas grill heated to medium-hot. At home you can grill a steak on the stovetop, using a heavy-duty grill pan. It makes a mess of the stovetop, because the grease splatters, but it cooks a pretty good steak.

We recommend using an instant-read thermometer to check the doneness. Rare steak will have an internal temperature of 120° to 125°F; medium-rare to medium should read 130° to 150°F. This should take somewhere near twenty minutes, depending upon the thickness of the meat and the heat. Above 150°F, a steak is considered well-done, which is not a desirable temperature for a really good steak! A steak should sit for five minutes or so before cutting, so remember that it will continue to cook as it sits when you gauge the internal temperature.

*Six 20-ounce prime rib-eye steaks, at room temperature*
*Sea salt and coarsely ground black pepper to taste*
*⅓ cup extra-virgin olive oil*
*Meat Butter (recipe follows)*

Clean, oil, and preheat the grill.

Wipe excess moisture from the exterior of the steaks using a paper towel. Season one side with salt and pepper.

Place the steaks on the hot grill, seasoned side down. Grill for 3 minutes. Season the top side and, using tongs, turn the steaks and grill for 3 minutes to just sear the exterior.

Remove the steaks from the grill and, using a pastry brush, lightly coat both sides of each steak with olive oil.

Return the steaks to the grill and cook, turning occasionally, until the exterior is nicely charred and the interior has reached the desired degree of doneness on an instant-read thermometer.

Remove from the grill and let rest for 5 minutes before serving with a generous pat of Meat Butter.

In *The Epicurean*, Charles Ranhofer names a 2-inch thick sirloin "*Bifteck de Contrefilet Delmonico au Beurre et aux Fines Herbes Cuites*." Chef Ranhofer flattened his steak to one and a half inches thick and required that it be twenty ounces in weight. He salted the raw meat, basted it with butter, and then broiled it over a moderate fire for fourteen minutes for very rare, eighteen minutes to be done "properly," and twenty-two minutes for well-done. He served it with "a little clear gravy" or "maître d'hôtel butter." This is, however, not what most people think of as a Delmonico Steak. Depending upon the butcher you speak to and the area of the country that you are from, a Delmonico Steak may be a bone-in top loin, boneless top sirloin, rib-eye, New York strip, or any number of other steaks. It is, however, generally described as a boneless steak cut from the short loin of a prime steer.

## MEAT BUTTER

*3 fresh bay leaves*

*1 tablespoon fresh thyme leaves*

*2 tablespoons sea salt*

*1 pound (4 sticks) unsalted butter, at room temperature*

Combine the bay leaves, thyme, and salt in a spice grinder and process until powdery.

Place the butter in a mixing bowl. Add the powdered mixture and, using a hand-held electric mixer, blend well.

Scrape the butter mixture onto the center of a sheet of plastic film. Pull the film up and over the soft butter and, using your hands, form the butter into a roll about 1¼ inches in diameter. Wrap tightly and refrigerate for up to 1 week, or wrap in freezer wrap, label, date, and freeze for up to 3 months.

When ready to serve, unwrap the flavored butter and, using a sharp knife, cut crosswise into ½-inch-thick slices, allowing one slice per steak.

# Tenderloin of Beef with Sweet Potato Croquettes

SERVES 6

The tenderloin of beef is the long main muscle in a short loin of beef. It is low in fat and—as the name suggests—extremely tender. When sold whole, it is often labeled chateaubriand, from which come tournedos and filet mignon steaks. One end of the muscle is quite thick, and it narrows down to an end that might be as much as three quarters less in diameter. We suggest that you buy the whole piece, as it is usually less expensive.

Croquettes of all types and sizes were featured on nineteenth-century menus, frequently as garnish for elaborate meat dishes. This recipe is almost identical to the one served at Delmonico's.

*5-pound whole tenderloin of beef, trimmed of all silver skin and fat*

*½ cup light olive oil*

*5 cloves garlic, peeled and smashed*

*¼ pound shallots, peeled and sliced*

*5 sprigs rosemary*

*5 sprigs thyme*

*2 bay leaves*

*¼ cup chopped flat-leaf parsley*

*1 tablespoon black peppercorns*

*Coarse salt and freshly ground pepper to taste*

*Sweet Potato Croquettes (recipe follows)*

*Fried Parsley, optional (see page 75)*

*1 cup Delmonico Original Steak Sauce or other steak sauce*

Trim both the thick end and the thin end from the tenderloin, leaving one piece that is fairly even in diameter and large enough to yield twelve ½-inch-thick slices. Reserve the trimmed meat for tartare (see page 80), kabobs, skewers, carpaccio, etc.

Loop a long piece of butcher's twine around one end of the loin and knot it, leaving a long string hanging. Working toward the other end of the loin, hold the long piece of twine about 1 inch from the knot against the meat. Loop the twine around the meat and bring it up though the 1-inch section to hold it stationary. Continue looping the twine in 1-inch sections until the entire tenderloin is held firmly, tying the final loop into a knot.

Place the tenderloin in a large glass baking dish or other nonporous container.

Combine the oil with the garlic and shallots in a small bowl. Stir in the rosemary, thyme, bay leaves, parsley, and peppercorns. Pour the oil mixture over the tenderloin. Cover and refrigerate for at least 8 hours or up to 2 days.

When ready to serve, preheat and oil the grill.

Remove the tenderloin from the marinade and, using a paper towel, carefully clean off any vegetables or herbs that cling to it. Season with salt and pepper and place on the hot grill.

Sear the meat, turning once or twice, for about 5 minutes, or until nicely marked on all sides. Then move it to a cooler spot on the grill and cook, turning occasionally, for about 20 minutes, or until an instant-read thermometer inserted into the thickest part registers 125°F for rare, 135°F for medium-rare, or 145°F for medium. Remove from the grill and let rest for 5 minutes before cutting. This allows the meat to increase another 5°F in temperature to finish cooking.

Untie the meat and, using a chef's knife, cut it crosswise into at least twelve ½-inch-thick slices. Lay the slices down the center of a warm serving platter and place the croquettes around the edge. Garnish with fried parsley, if desired, and serve with steak sauce on the side.

# SWEET POTATO CROQUETTES

*2 pounds sweet potatoes, well washed and dried*

*3 large egg yolks*

*2 tablespoons unsalted butter, softened*

*Freshly grated nutmeg to taste*

*Coarse salt and freshly ground white pepper to taste*

*2 cups all-purpose flour*

*2 large whole eggs*

*2 tablespoons cream*

*4 cups fresh bread crumbs*

*6 cups canola oil*

Preheat the oven to 375°F.

Lightly rub the skins of the potatoes with a bit of oil and bake them for about 45 minutes, or until the point of a small, sharp knife can easily be inserted in the center.

Remove the potatoes from the oven and set aside until cool enough to handle.

When cool enough to handle, split the potatoes open. Using a tablespoon, scoop out the flesh and place it in a mixing bowl. Beat in the egg yolks, butter, nutmeg, salt, and pepper. When smooth, cover and refrigerate for 1 hour.

Place the flour in a shallow bowl. Season with salt and pepper.

Combine the eggs and cream in another shallow bowl.

Place the bread crumbs in a third shallow bowl. Season with salt and pepper.

Line one baking sheet with parchment paper and another with a double layer of paper towel.

Form the chilled potato mixture into cylinders about 2 inches long and 1½ inches in diameter. Roll each ball in the seasoned flour, followed by the egg mixture, and then in the seasoned bread crumbs. Place the coated balls on the parchment-lined baking sheet.

Heat the oil to 375°F in a deep-fat fryer.

Carefully drop the balls into the hot fat, a few at a time, and fry for about 3 minutes, or until golden and crisp. Using a slotted spoon, carefully transfer the croquettes to the paper-towel-lined baking sheet to drain.

If necessary, place the drained croquettes on a baking sheet in a preheated 200°F oven to keep warm until serving.

# Tenderloin Hash

SERVES 6

Hash was always a great lunch favorite among men. Charles Ranhofer even attached the names of favored gentlemen to two of his versions, Hash à la Sam Ward (a famous bon vivant of the period—his sister, Julia, was the author of "The Battle Hymn of the Republic") and Hash à la Shepler. Hash really is nothing more than a very tasty way to use leftover meat, usually corned beef or roast beef, although it can be made from almost anything, including vegetables.

*3 cups diced cooked tenderloin of beef*

*3 cups diced cooked potatoes*

*2 tablespoons chopped flat-leaf parsley*

*2 tablespoons unsalted butter*

*¾ cup finely diced onions*

*½ cup cream or leftover gravy*

*Coarse salt and freshly ground pepper to taste*

Preheat the oven to 350°F.

Combine the beef, potatoes, and parsley in a mixing bowl, tossing to blend well. Set aside.

Melt the butter in a large cast-iron frying pan (or other heavy ovenproof skillet) over medium heat. Add the onions and sauté for about 5 minutes, or until nicely colored. Add the meat mixture, stirring to combine well. Pour the cream or gravy over all and stir to blend. Season with salt and pepper. Pat the mixture down into the pan, smoothing the top with a spatula.

Bake the hash for about 25 minutes, or until nicely browned and crusty.

Remove from the oven and let stand for 5 minutes, then cut into portions and serve with a green salad.

# Veal Sweetbreads with Morels and Fava Beans and Golden Raisin Purée

SERVES 6

Sweetbreads are infrequently cooked at home, probably because they take some time to prepare. However, since much of the preparation can be done ahead of time, we think that they make a wonderful dinner party dish. They were extremely popular in the late 1800s, when they were prepared in many different, elaborate ways. We think that this preparation reflects that early extravagance.

> *3 pounds veal sweetbreads (see note)*
>
> *3 tablespoons coarse salt, plus more to taste*
>
> *¼ cup white vinegar*
>
> *1 cup Wondra flour (see page 75)*
>
> *Freshly ground pepper to taste*
>
> *¼ cup clarified butter*
>
> *½ cup diced carrots, blanched*
>
> *½ cup diced onions*
>
> *½ cup diced leeks*
>
> *½ cup diced, crisply cooked bacon*
>
> *¼ cup vermouth*
>
> *1 cup veal stock*
>
> *½ cup very small morels*
>
> *½ cup fresh fava beans (see note)*
>
> *Golden Raisin Purée (recipe follows)*

Place the sweetbreads in cold water to cover. Add 1 tablespoon of salt, cover, and refrigerate for at least 2 hours or up to 24 hours.

Rinse the soaked sweetbreads under cold running water, then place them in a heavy saucepan with cold water to cover. Add the vinegar, along with 2 tablespoons of salt, and bring to a boil over medium-high heat. Lower the heat, simmer for 14 minutes, then drain well. Place the sweetbreads in a fine-mesh sieve and rinse under cold, running water for 5 minutes.

Place a clean kitchen towel on a platter. Set aside.

Using a small, sharp knife, carefully trim any sinew, veins, and fat from the sweetbreads. Divide the lobes into 6 equal portions, keeping the pieces as large as possible. Place the pieces on the towel-lined platter and cover with another clean kitchen towel. Invert another platter over the sweetbreads and place a heavy weight on top, such as a large can of tomatoes. Refrigerate for 12 hours.

Combine the flour with salt and pepper in a large, shallow bowl.

Remove the sweetbreads from the refrigerator. Uncover and lightly dust each piece with the seasoned flour.

Heat 2 tablespoons of the clarified butter in a large, nonstick sauté pan over medium-high heat. Add the sweetbreads and sear, turning occasionally, for about 4 minutes or until nicely browned.

Transfer the sweetbreads to a double layer of paper towel to drain.

Return the pan to medium heat. Add the carrots, onions, leeks, and bacon and sauté for 2 minutes. Add the vermouth and cook, stirring constantly with a wooden spoon to scrape any brown bits up from the bottom of the pan.

Add the stock, along with salt and pepper, raise the heat, and bring to a boil. Add the sweetbreads and lower the heat to a simmer. Simmer for about 10 minutes, or until the sauce has reduced by half.

Preheat the oven to 200°F.

Remove the sweetbreads from the heat and, using a slotted spoon, transfer them to a plate. Strain the sweetbread cooking liquid through a fine-mesh sieve into a clean saucepan, separately reserving the solids. Keep the sauce warm until ready to use.

Heat 1 tablespoon of the remaining clarified butter in a large sauté pan over high heat. Add the morels and favas, along with the reserved vegetables. Season with salt and pepper and cook, stirring frequently, for about 3 minutes, or until heated through.

Heat the remaining clarified butter in a clean sauté pan over high heat. Add the sweetbreads and sear, turning once, for about 3 minutes, or until nicely crisped on both sides.

Spoon two equal portions of the raisin purée on the side of each of 6 dinner plates. Place an equal portion of the morel mixture in the center of the plates and then place a portion of the sweetbreads on top of the vegetables. Spoon some of the reserved sauce around the edge of each plate and serve.

Sweetbreads are the thymus glands of veal, young beef, lamb, or pork. The longest gland is a lobe in the throat, and the fuller lobe is located near the animal's heart. The fuller lobe from a veal calf is the most prized for its delicate flavor and creaminess. Sometimes sweetbreads are soaked in milk to add even more creaminess when cooked.

Fresh fava beans have a very tough outer skin that must be removed before cooking. Dried fava beans are not an acceptable replacement.

### GOLDEN RAISIN PURÉE

> *2 cups golden raisins*
> *1 cup Muscat, Sauternes, or other pale sweet wine*
> *¼ cup apple cider*
> *2 teaspoons vanilla extract*

Combine the raisins with the wine, cider, and vanilla in a small nonreactive saucepan over medium-low heat. Bring to a simmer and cook for about 12 minutes, or until the liquid is reduced to about 2 tablespoons.

Transfer the mixture to a blender and process to a thick purée. Serve at room temperature.

# Herb-Roasted Rack of Lamb

SERVES 6

Early Delmonico's recipes separate lamb from mutton, with recipes using parts ranging from trotters to saddles. Strongly flavored mutton is almost unobtainable today, and the lamb that we do get is usually very young and tender. We only use superb Colorado lamb at the restaurant simply because we think that it is the tenderest, most flavorful lamb available.

*Three 1½-pound baby lamb racks*

*1 cup light olive oil*

*1 shallot, peeled and sliced*

*1 clove garlic, peeled and sliced*

*1 tablespoon fresh rosemary leaves*

*1 tablespoon fresh thyme leaves*

*1 tablespoon cracked black pepper*

*1 cup fresh bread crumbs*

*2 teaspoons dried lavender*

*1 teaspoon dried oregano*

*1 teaspoon dried rosemary*

*Coarse salt and freshly ground pepper*

*2 tablespoons canola oil*

*½ cup whole-grain mustard*

Place the lamb racks in a baking dish large enough to hold them comfortably. Alternatively, place them in an extra-large resealable plastic bag.

Combine the olive oil, shallot, and garlic with the fresh rosemary, thyme, and cracked pepper. Pour the seasoned oil over the lamb, tossing to coat. Either cover the dish or seal the bag and refrigerate for 2 days.

Combine the bread crumbs with the dried lavender, oregano, and rosemary in a large, shallow bowl. Season with just a bit of salt and pepper. Set aside.

When ready to roast, preheat the oven to 400°F.

Remove the lamb from the marinade and pat dry. Season with salt and pepper.

Heat the canola oil in a large ovenproof sauté pan over medium-high heat. Add the lamb, flesh side down, and sear, turning occasionally, for about 4 minutes, or until nicely colored.

Remove the lamb from the pan and, using a pastry brush, generously coat the flesh with the mustard. Then roll the lamb in the seasoned bread crumbs.

Roast the lamb for about 20 minutes, or until an instant-read thermometer inserted into the thickest part reads 135°F for rare or 145°F for medium.

Remove from the oven and allow to rest for 5 minutes before cutting into chops. Serve 4 chops per person with any starch or vegetable you desire. We like our great hash browns (see page 117) and some caramelized Brussels sprouts (simply 2 pints of baby Brussels sprouts cooked in ¼ cup butter and a touch of brown sugar).

# Pork Cutlets with Apple Fritters

SERVES 6

This recipe is almost exactly the same as a recipe for *Côtelettes de Porc aux Croquettes de Pommes d'Arbes* created by Charles Ranhofer in the 1880s. We think it perfect for the contemporary table, particularly when made with the flavorful heirloom pork now available at farmers' markets and quality butchers. The cutlets would be just fine served on their own with a bit of fresh lemon to accent their crispy coating.

> *Six 1-inch-thick, bone-in pork chops*
>
> *3 large eggs, beaten*
>
> *1 tablespoon freshly grated Parmesan cheese*
>
> *1 tablespoon chopped flat-leaf parsley*
>
> *Coarse salt and freshly ground pepper*
>
> *2 cups seasoned bread crumbs*
>
> *1 cup olive oil*
>
> *Apple Fritters (recipe follows)*
>
> *Red Onion Preserves (recipe follows)*

Place the pork chops on a clean work surface. Using a chef's knife, trim off all the fat. Using a filet knife, cut from the bone out, laterally dividing the meat in half without cutting completely through. You want to be able to open the meat out in one piece from the bone. Using your fingertips, push the meat down to flatten it.

Cover one chop with plastic film and, using a meat mallet, pound it out to make a ¼-inch-thick cutlet still attached to the bone. Continue flattening until all the cutlets are prepared.

Combine the eggs, cheese, and parsley in a shallow bowl. Season with a pinch of salt and pepper.

Place the bread crumbs on a plate.

Line a baking sheet with a double layer of paper towel.

Dip each cutlet into the egg mixture and then pat it down into the bread crumbs to cover both sides.

Heat the oil in a large frying pan over high heat. When it is shimmering, add the pork, one piece at a time, and fry, turning once, for about 4 minutes, or until cooked through and golden brown. Carefully transfer to the paper towel-lined baking sheet to drain. (You must control the oil temperature while frying by lowering the heat when removing the pork and then raising it to shimmering before adding another piece. If the oil has too many browned bits, pour it off and start with fresh oil.

Place a pork cutlet on each of 6 dinner plates. Garnish with Apple Fritters and a spoon of Red Onion Preserves. Serve immediately.

## APPLE FRITTERS

*2 tablespoons unsalted butter*

*3 apples, peeled, cored, and diced*

*2 tablespoons light brown sugar*

*¼ teaspoon ground cinnamon*

*2 tablespoons raisins*

*2 tablespoons slivered toasted almonds or chopped toasted walnuts or pecans*

*2 tablespoons fig jam or cherry jam*

*1 cup all-purpose flour*

*2 large eggs, beaten*

*1¼ cups fresh bread crumbs*

*4 cups vegetable oil*

*¼ cup confectioners' sugar, for dusting*

Heat the butter in a large sauté pan over medium heat. Add the apples and sauté for 5 minutes. Sprinkle with the brown sugar and cinnamon and continue to cook for another minute, or until the sugar has dissolved. Add the raisins and nuts, stirring to combine. Cook for another 2 to 3 minutes, or until the mixture is well blended. Remove from the heat and allow to cool.

Scrape the apple mixture into a mixing bowl. Add the jam and, using your hands, squeeze the mixture together to make a smooth paste.

Line a baking sheet with parchment paper. Set aside.

Line a baking sheet with a double layer of paper towel. Set aside.

Place the flour, eggs, and bread crumbs in separate shallow bowls, setting them in a straight line.

Form the apple mixture into 1½-inch round balls and place them on the parchment-lined baking sheet.

Dip each ball into the flour, then the egg, and finally into the bread crumbs. Then, using the palms of your hands, roll the ball into a little cylinder or football shape. Return the coated cylinders to the parchment-lined baking sheet.

Heat the oil to 375°F in a deep-fat fryer.

Add the apple cylinders, a few at a time, and fry for about 45 seconds, or until golden brown. Using a slotted spoon, transfer the fritters to the paper-towel-lined baking sheet and continue frying until all the fritters are done.

Sprinkle with confectioners' sugar and serve warm. If necessary, place in a preheated 200°F oven to keep warm until ready to serve.

### RED ONION PRESERVES

> *2 tablespoons unsalted butter*
>
> *2 large red onions, peeled, trimmed, and thinly sliced crosswise*
>
> *½ cup sugar*
>
> *1 cup dry red wine*
>
> *¼ cup red wine vinegar*
>
> *2 tablespoons grenadine syrup, optional*

Heat the butter in a large sauté pan over medium heat. Add the onions and cook, stirring frequently, for about 5 minutes, or until the onions have begun to sweat their liquid. Stir in the sugar. Add the wine and vinegar, raise the heat, and bring to a boil. Immediately lower the heat and cook at a bare simmer for about 20 minutes, or until almost all of the liquid has evaporated. Stir in the grenadine, if using, and cook for another 3 minutes.

Scrape the preserves from the pan into a clean container. If not using immediately, cover and refrigerate for up to 1 week.

# Crown Roast of Pork with Sausage Stuffing

SERVES 6 TO 10

There is no meat dish more elegant than a crown roast. The base can be either pork or lamb, with each offering its own particular charm. This pork presentation is almost exactly the same as one prepared for banquets in the early days of Delmonico's. The stuffing is a simple but rich traditional mix that marries perfectly with the subtle flavor of the pork. Most butchers will trim and tie the racks into the crown shape.

> One 8- to 10-pound crown roast of pork
>
> Sausage Stuffing (recipe follows)
>
> ¼ cup canola oil
>
> Coarse salt and freshly ground pepper to taste
>
> ½ cup dry white wine
>
> 1 cup chicken broth
>
> ¼ cup orange juice
>
> 2 tablespoons cornstarch dissolved in 2 tablespoons cold water
>
> 1 tablespoon chopped flat-leaf parsley

Preheat the oven to 450°F.

Place the tied roast in the center of a large roasting pan. Carefully fill the center with the stuffing, patting down slightly to fill the cavity completely without compacting it.

Using small pieces of aluminum foil, cover the bare bones to keep them from burning during roasting.

Using a pastry brush, lightly coat the exterior of the roast and the top of the stuffing with oil. Season the exterior with salt and pepper and roast for 20 minutes. Reduce the heat to 300°F and roast for an additional 2½ hours, or until an instant-read thermometer inserted into the thickest part of the meat reads 160°F. If the stuffing gets too brown and dry, brush the surface with oil and cover with a piece of aluminum foil.

Remove the roast from the oven and carefully transfer it to a serving platter. Let rest for 15 minutes before cutting. (Note that the internal temperature of the meat will continue to rise as the meat rests.)

Place the roasting pan on the stovetop over medium heat. Add the wine and bring to a boil, scraping up the browned bits from the bottom of the pan. When the wine has reduced slightly and the browned pieces are incorporated into it, remove the pan from the heat and transfer the mixture to a saucepan over medium-high heat. Add the broth and orange

juice, bring to a boil, then lower the heat and simmer for 10 minutes, or until reduced by one third. Whisk in the cornstarch mixture and cook, whisking constantly, for a couple of minutes, or until thickened. Add the parsley and season with salt and pepper.

Present the roast at the table. Carve it into chops and serve with the stuffing and gravy.

### SAUSAGE STUFFING

*12 cups dried white and whole-wheat bread cubes*

*½ cup (1 stick) unsalted butter*

*1 cup diced onion*

*¼ cup finely diced celery*

*1 tablespoon minced flat-leaf parsley*

*1 pound pork sausage meat, crumbled*

*1½ cups dried cranberries or cherries*

*1 cup chopped walnuts*

*½ cup golden raisins*

*Approximately 2 cups chicken broth or stock*

*2 teaspoons minced fresh sage*

*1½ teaspoons minced fresh thyme*

*1 teaspoon minced fresh marjoram*

*Coarse salt and freshly ground pepper to taste*

Place the bread cubes in a large mixing bowl. Set aside.

Heat the butter in a large frying pan over medium heat. Add the onion, celery, and parsley and cook, stirring frequently, for about 5 minutes, or until the vegetables have softened but are not browned. Add the sausage and fry, stirring frequently, for 10 minutes, or until cooked. Add the cranberries (or cherries), walnuts, and raisins and sauté for 5 minutes. Add ½ cup of the broth along with the sage, thyme, and marjoram, stirring to blend.

Scrape the mixture into the bread cubes, tossing to combine. Add enough of the remaining broth to make a moist, but not wet mixture. Season with salt and pepper. If not using immediately, cover with plastic film and refrigerate until ready to use.

When ready to use, bring to room temperature before stuffing the roast.

# Venison Medallions with Ginger Cranberry Sauce

SERVES 6

Once only available during hunting season, venison is now farm-raised in New Zealand and the United States and is available all year long. However, people mostly seem to cook it in the fall, due perhaps to its rich flavor. It is lower in fat, cholesterol, and calories than beef and is extremely tender when properly prepared. This is a simple dish that makes a wonderful dinner-party entrée.

*Six 5-ounce, ¾-inch-thick venison medallions*

*Coarse salt and freshly ground pepper to taste*

*2 tablespoons canola oil*

*2 small shallots, peeled and minced*

*1 cup fresh cranberries*

*1 teaspoon freshly grated ginger*

*1 cup dry red wine*

*½ cup Champagne vinegar*

*1 cup veal demi-glace (see page 173)*

*2 tablespoons pure maple syrup*

*1½ tablespoons chopped chives*

Preheat the oven to low.

Season the venison with salt and pepper.

Heat the oil in a large sauté pan over high heat. Add the venison and sear for about 90 seconds, or until the bottom is browned. Turn the meat and sear the remaining side for 2 minutes, or until well colored but still rare in the center. Transfer the venison to a baking dish and tent lightly with aluminum foil to keep warm.

Return the pan to medium heat. Add the shallots and sauté for 2 minutes. Stir in the cranberries and ginger and continue to cook, stirring frequently, for another 2 minutes. Add the wine and vinegar and stir to deglaze the pan. Raise the heat and bring to a boil, then adjust the temperature and cook at a high simmer for about 10 minutes, or until the liquid has reduced to ½ cup. Add the demi-glace and maple syrup and season with salt and pepper. Again bring to a boil, then lower the heat and cook at a high simmer for about 10 minutes, or until a saucelike consistency is achieved. Taste and, if necessary, season with salt and pepper.

Five minutes before the sauce is ready, transfer the venison to the warm oven.

Spoon a small amount of sauce in the center of each of 6 dinner plates. Place a venison medallion on top and spoon more sauce over the meat and around the plate. Sprinkle with chives and serve.

It would have been unimaginable to serve something as unadorned as the simple grilled chicken breast popular today in the early days of Delmonico's. Almost every poultry dish that we have found was heavily sauced, garnished, and stuffed. Whether domestic or wild, capon, chicken, turkey, squab, duck, quinea fowl, goose, and pigeon were all considered poultry, with chicken and pullet (a young hen) most often featured on the early menus. Generally only duck appeared on the menu for the more elegant, many-coursed dinners.

# Poultry and Game Birds

DEVILED CHICKEN LEGS

ROAST CHICKEN WITH
ROOT VEGETABLE POT PIE

CHICKEN BREASTS LORENZO

SEARED CORNISH GAME HENS
WITH PORCINI GRAVY

TURKEY ROULADE WITH CHESTNUT STUFFING

FRENCH BREAST OF PHEASANT
WITH BUTTERNUT SQUASH RISOTTO

SQUAB WITH FOIE GRAS BRAISED CABBAGE

DUCK BREASTS WITH PEAR PURÉE,
SWISS CHARD, AND DRIED CHERRY SAUCE

One of our favorite chicken dishes from an old menu is *Poulets Sautés à la Montesquieu*. The instructions for its preparation (here given in a very much simplified version) say to make a standing openwork border of cooked paste (pastry dough) one inch in from the edge of the entrée plate, then spread it out slightly, brush it with an egg wash, and set it aside to dry. A wooden bottom is positioned in the center of the plate and covered with a very thin layer of cooked paste. Then the legs and breasts are cut from three chickens using an elaborate method. Some of the breast meat is larded and cooked in butter and fat pork. Other pieces are stuffed with a cream forcemeat and poached. Gashes are cut into the breast tenders (at least that's what we think they were) and stuffed with truffles. The legs are boned and stuffed with forcemeat and mushroom duxelle and cooked in butter, fat pork, and chicken stock. Finally, everything is glazed and formed into a mold that fits into the paste border. A velouté sauce and more truffles complete the dish. Today, we are content to always have a straightforward chicken dish on the menu and only rarely offer other birds as specials.

# Deviled Chicken Legs

We found this recipe in a trove of Delmonico's specialties. Although we had seen deviled beef bones, we had never seen a recipe for deviled chicken legs. We decided to try a contemporary version to offer on our bar menu. This devil can be as hot or as mild as you like. We like ours a bit spicy—and cooled down with an ice-cold New York lager.

*12 chicken legs, skin removed*

*1 tablespoon coarse salt*

*½ tablespoon coarsely ground black pepper*

*½ tablespoon garlic powder*

*Juice of 1½ lemons*

*6 tablespoons mayonnaise*

*3 tablespoons Dijon mustard*

*1½ tablespoons hot pepper sauce of choice*

*1 tablespoon prepared horseradish, well drained*

*1 tablespoon Worcestershire sauce*

*1 teaspoon cayenne pepper*

*1 teaspoon smoked paprika*

*1¼ cups Italian seasoned bread crumbs*

*⅓ cup chopped flat-leaf parsley*

Preheat the oven to 375°F.

Rinse the chicken legs under cold running water. Pat dry.

Combine the salt, pepper, and garlic powder. Season the legs with this mixture and place them in a large, shallow container.

Combine the lemon juice, mayonnaise, mustard, hot pepper sauce, horseradish, Worcestershire sauce, cayenne, and paprika in a mixing bowl. When well-blended, pour the mixture over the chicken legs and toss to coat well.

Combine the bread crumbs and parsley in a large shallow bowl.

Roll each chicken leg in the bread crumbs. Place the coated legs in a single layer on a nonstick baking pan.

When all the legs have been coated, bake them for about 50 minutes, or until the juices run clear and the legs are golden and crisp.

Remove from the oven and serve hot.

# Roast Chicken with Root Vegetable Pot Pie

SERVES 6

This is a current customer favorite at Delmonico's. The chicken offers an alternative to the large, juicy steaks, while the presentation is in the opulent style of the early restaurant menu. Although you can certainly serve the chicken on its own, for the convenience of the home cook the pot pie can be put together a day or so before and the jus can be made early in the day. The chicken can be seared a couple of hours ahead of time, then finished in the oven so that everything can be quickly put together at the last minute.

> *Three 3-pound free-range chickens*
> *Juice of 2 lemons*
> *¾ cup light olive oil*
> *4 sprigs rosemary*
> *3 cloves garlic, peeled and chopped*
> *1 large onion, peeled and chopped*
> *2 tablespoons fresh thyme leaves*
> *6 tablespoons unsalted butter*
> *¼ cup canola oil*
> *Coarse salt and freshly ground pepper to taste*
> *6 Root Vegetable Pot Pies (see page 112)*
> *6 sprigs rosemary*
> *Chicken Jus (recipe follows)*

Place the chickens in a large pot of cold salted water and let brine for 1 hour. Drain and rinse well under cold running water.

Using a very sharp chef's knife, cut each chicken in half through the back and directly down the center between the breasts.

Using a boning knife, clip the wing at the first joint, leaving the shoulder bone attached. Reserve the first joint. Run the knife in a circle around the shoulder bone closest to the breast to loosen the meat. Then, using the knife, scrape the meat down and off the bone. Using a kitchen towel, clean the bone of any residual meat. This is called Frenching the bone.

Turn each chicken half skin side down and, using a boning knife, remove the breast bone by slipping the knife between the bone and the flesh and pushing slightly against the bone as you cut along the bone to its end.

Make an incision down the center of the flesh closest to the thigh bone. Slit down to open up the thigh. Using your fingertip along with the knife, feel

around the bone and loosen it from the flesh. Remove the thigh bone. Reserve the breast and thigh bones along with the first joints of the wings.

Leaving the boneless thigh attached to the breast, clip off the legs just beneath the thigh-leg joint. French the meat from the legs as you did for the wings.

Place the boned chicken halves in a glass baking dish.

Combine the lemon juice, oil, rosemary, garlic, onion, and thyme in a small mixing bowl. When well blended, pour the mixture over the chicken. Cover and refrigerate for at least 1 hour or up to 8 hours.

When ready to cook, preheat the oven to 400°F.

Generously coat a large nonstick baking dish with 2 tablespoons of the butter. Set aside.

Heat a large sauté pan over high heat. Add 2 tablespoons each of the butter and the canola oil. Add half of the chicken pieces, skin side down. Season with salt and pepper and sear, turning once, for about 5 minutes or until nicely browned.

Transfer the chicken to the prepared baking dish. Repeat with the remaining butter, oil, and chicken pieces. When transferring the chicken to the baking dish, take care not to overlap any of the pieces.

Roast the chicken for about 10 minutes, or until an instant-read thermometer inserted into the thickest part reads 155°F.

Place a Root Vegetable Pot Pie on each of 6 dinner plates. Nestle a chicken breast and a leg on top of the pie. Garnish with a sprig of rosemary and drizzle the jus around the plate. Serve immediately.

## Chicken Jus

*¼ cup (1 stick) unsalted butter, at room temperature*
*2 cloves garlic, peeled and chopped*
*1 onion, peeled and sliced*
*1 cup dry red wine*
*2 tablespoons Wondra flour (see page 75)*
*1 cup chicken stock or fat-free broth*
*1 cup beef stock or fat-free broth*
*Reserved chicken bones from Roast Chicken preparation*
*Coarse salt and freshly ground pepper to taste*
*2 tablespoon chopped mixed herbs such as flat-leaf parsley, chives, and tarragon*

Heat 2 tablespoons of the butter in a medium saucepan over medium heat. Add the garlic and onion and sauté for about 4 minutes or until the vegetables have sweated their liquid. Add the red wine, raise the heat, and bring the mixture to a boil. Lower the heat and simmer for about 7 minutes or until reduced to ¼ cup.

Slowly add the flour, whisking until well incorporated. Cook, whisking constantly, for 1 minute. Add the chicken and beef stocks, along with the chicken bones, raise the heat, and bring to a boil. Season with salt and pepper and lower the heat. Simmer for about 20 minutes, or until reduced by half.

Remove the pan from the heat and strain the jus through a fine-mesh sieve into a clean saucepan, discarding the solids.

Return the gravy to medium heat and bring it to a simmer. Lower the heat and, whisking constantly, beat in the remaining 2 tablespoons of butter. Fold in the herbs and serve.

If not using immediately, do not add the herbs. Transfer to a covered container and refrigerate for up to 2 days. Reheat and add the herbs before serving.

# Chicken Breasts Lorenzo

SERVES 6

A small tribute to Lorenzo Delmonico, one of the most distinguished restaurateurs America has ever seen. The elegance of this simple but luxurious dish epitomizes his courtliness and polish. This is a wonderful dish for entertaining as the sauce and stuffing can be made well in advance of use. The breasts can be stuffed in the morning and finished at dinner time.

*3 tablespoons truffle butter (see notes)*

*2 shallots, peeled and chopped*

*1 clove garlic, peeled and minced*

*¼ cup finely diced leeks*

*½ pound black trumpet mushrooms, cleaned and sliced*

*½ pound chanterelles, cleaned and sliced*

*Coarse salt and freshly ground pepper to taste*

*6 tablespoons foie gras mousse (see page 66)*

*2 tablespoons unsalted butter or truffle butter, at room temperature*

*2 tablespoons truffle oil (see page 119)*

*6 chicken breast halves, skin and wings on*

*2 tablespoons canola oil*

*Celery-Onion Confit (recipe follows)*

*Herbed Chicken Sauce (recipe follows)*

*6 sprigs rosemary*

Heat the truffle butter in a medium sauté pan over medium-low heat. Add the shallots, garlic, and leeks and sauté for about 4 minutes, or until the vegetables have sweated their liquid but not taken on any color. Raise the heat and, when the pan is sizzling, add the mushrooms, stirring to combine. Season with salt and pepper, lower the heat, and sauté for another 5 minutes, or until the mushrooms have wilted and exuded their moisture. Remove from the heat and allow to cool.

When the mushroom mixture is cool, transfer it to a chopping block. Using a chef's knife, finely chop the mix. Measure out and set aside 6 tablespoons, reserving the remainder for garnish.

Combine the mousse, butter, and truffle oil in a small mixing bowl. Using a rubber spatula, work the ingredients together. When blended, add the reserved 6 tablespoons of the mushroom mixture, again working together to blend. Taste and, if necessary, season with salt and pepper. Set aside.

Using a small, sharp knife, clip the wing at the first joint, leaving the shoulder bone attached. Reserve the first joint. Run the knife in a circle around the

Lorenzo Delmonico's day was strictly divided. He understood that no matter how masterly a restaurant's service, its success in the long run depends on the quality of its food. Every day at four o'clock in the morning, he would go to the Washington and Fulton markets and pick out "what was good and fine, from meats and game, fish, fowl, terrapin, whatever was in season, and all that makes a fine table beautiful." At eight o'clock he returned to his restaurant in a cab, followed by others loaded with his purchases. He would drink a cup of black coffee and smoke a "Figaro cigar," then take a cab home and go to bed. "Every evening he came back, and sat with his friends [customers], after taking a little supper, till twelve o'clock." A report from an employee as quoted by Lately Thomas in *Delmonico's: A Century of Splendor*.

This was Lorenzo's daily devotion to Delmonico's for more than twenty-five years.

shoulder bone closest to the breast to loosen the meat. Then, using the knife, scrape the meat down and off the bone. Using a kitchen towel, clean the bone of any residual meat. This is called Frenching the bone.

Working from the top of the breast, make an incision in the exact center of the flesh and slide the knife about three quarters of the way in and down from one end to the other to form a pocket.

Carefully stuff about 2 tablespoons of the mousse mixture into the pocket, taking care to pack it evenly over the entire pocket opening. Transfer the stuffed breasts to a platter, cover with plastic film, and refrigerate for 1 hour to harden the stuffing.

Preheat the oven to 400°F.

Season the chicken with salt and pepper.

Heat the canola oil in a large, ovenproof sauté pan over medium-high heat until very hot, but not smoking. Add the breasts, skin side down, and sear, shaking the pan from time to time, for about 5 minutes, or until nicely browned. Turn the breasts and sear the remaining side for 4 minutes.

Transfer the pan to the preheated oven and roast for about 10 minutes, or until an instant-read thermometer inserted into the thickest part reads 155°F.

Remove the pan from the oven and let the breasts rest for 5 minutes before cutting.

Using a chef's knife, cut each breast on the diagonal into 3 equal pieces. Slightly fan the meat out on each of 6 dinner plates. Place a large quenelle (see note) of the confit next to the chicken on each plate. Drizzle Herbed Chicken Sauce over the chicken and around the plate. Garnish with fresh herbs and serve.

### NOTES:

A quenelle is both a small oval-shaped poached dumpling and the oval shape itself. To form the perfect oval shape, scoop up a heaping teaspoon of the mixture, place another teaspoon on top of the mix, and then roll it back and forth to make an evenly shaped oval. It may be helpful to wet the spoons for ease of movement.

Truffle butter, foie gras mousse, and truffle oil are all available at specialty food stores or online (see sources).

### CELERY-ONION CONFIT

*6 cups chopped celery*

*4 cups diced Maui or other sweet onion*

*3 cups diced fennel bulb*

*Peel of 1 orange, cut into thin strips*

*2 cups olive oil*

*Coarse salt and freshly ground pepper to taste*

Combine the celery, onion, fennel, and orange zest in a large, heavy-bottom saucepan. Drizzle the oil over the top and season with salt and pepper. Place over medium heat and bring to a simmer. Cook for about 45 minutes, or until the vegetables are very soft.

Remove from the heat and pour into a fine-mesh sieve. Allow to drain for about 15 minutes, pushing on the solids from time to time to extract most of the oil. (You can reserve the liquid for use in vinaigrettes, salad dressings, soups, or stews.)

Transfer the solids to the bowl of a food processor fitted with the metal blade. Pulse, using quick on and off turns, to make a slightly textured mix.

Scrape the confit from the bowl into a clean container. If not using immediately, cover and refrigerate for up to 1 week. Bring to room temperature before serving.

## HERBED CHICKEN SAUCE

*2 tablespoons canola oil*

*2 cloves garlic, peeled and chopped*

*1 large onion, peeled and sliced*

*2 cups dry red wine*

*1 bay leaf*

*1 tablespoon black peppercorns*

*2 cups chicken stock or fat-free broth*

*2 cups beef stock or fat-free broth*

*Coarse salt and freshly ground pepper to taste*

*¼ cup (½ stick) unsalted butter, at room temperature*

*2 tablespoons heavy cream, at room temperature*

*2 tablespoons chopped mixed herbs such as flat-leaf parsley, chives, and tarragon*

Heat the oil in a medium saucepan over medium heat. Add the garlic and onion and sauté for about 4 minutes, or until the vegetables have sweated their liquid. Add the red wine, bay leaf, and peppercorns. Raise the heat and bring to a boil, then lower the temperature and simmer for about 7 minutes, or until reduced to ¼ cup.

Add the chicken and beef stocks, and return the liquid to a boil. Season with salt and pepper and lower the heat to a simmer for about 20 minutes, or until reduced to 1½ cups.

Remove the pan from the heat and strain the jus through a fine-mesh sieve into a clean saucepan, discarding the solids.

Return the sauce to medium heat and bring to a simmer. Lower the heat and, whisking constantly, beat in the butter, followed by the cream. Taste and, if necessary, season with salt and pepper. Fold in the herbs and serve.

If not using immediately, do not add the herbs. Transfer to a covered container and refrigerate for up to 2 days. Reheat and add the herbs before serving.

# Seared Cornish Game Hens
# with Porcini Gravy

SERVES 6

This simple recipe makes a wonderful Sunday night supper—and the gravy works wonders with mashed potatoes. The marinated birds can also be cooked on a grill. The skin won't achieve the crispness that it does in the oven, but the birds will still be moist and tender. The recipe can be made equally well with small chickens.

*2 cups light olive oil*

*5 shallots, peeled and sliced*

*4 cloves garlic, peeled and sliced*

*2 bay leaves*

*2 tablespoons chopped fresh thyme*

*2 tablespoons chopped fresh sage*

*2 tablespoons chopped flat-leaf parsley*

*1 tablespoon black peppercorns*

*6 Cornish game hens, split in half lengthwise*

*¼ cup (½ stick) unsalted butter, at room temperature*

*Coarse salt and freshly ground pepper to taste*

*Porcini Gravy (recipe follows)*

Combine 1 cup of the oil with the shallots, garlic, bay leaves, chopped herbs, and peppercorns in an extra-large resealable plastic bag. Add the split hens and seal. Shake the bag to distribute the marinade. Refrigerate for at least 8 hours or up to 24 hours.

Preheat the oven to 375°F. Using 2 tablespoons of butter for each pan, generously butter 2 baking trays. Set aside.

Remove the hens from the marinade. Using paper towels, pat the excess marinade from the birds. Generously season with salt and pepper.

Heat ¼ cup of oil in each of 2 nonstick frying pans over high heat. Place 3 hen halves in each pan, skin side down. Sear for about 5 minutes, or until nicely browned. Using tongs, transfer the hens, skin side down, to the prepared baking trays.

Wipe the pans clean with paper towels. Return them to high heat, add ¼ cup fresh oil to each one, and repeat the above process with the remaining birds.

When all the hens have been seared, transfer the baking trays to the preheated oven and roast for 12 minutes, or until the juices run clear and the skin is golden brown and crispy.

Using tongs, transfer the hens to a serving platter. Serve hot with Porcini Gravy on the side.

## PORCINI GRAVY

*2 ounces dried porcini mushrooms*

*1 cup fat-free chicken broth*

*1 cup fat-free beef broth, heated*

*2 tablespoons unsalted butter*

*3 shallots, peeled and minced*

*1 clove garlic, peeled and minced*

*½ cup dry white wine*

*1 tablespoon Wondra flour (see page 75)*

*5 black peppercorns*

*2 allspice berries*

*Coarse salt to taste*

*¼ cup heavy cream*

*Freshly ground pepper to taste*

*2 tablespoons chopped mixed fresh herbs such as parsley, sage, thyme, and chives*

Combine the porcini with the hot broths in a heatproof bowl. Set aside to rehydrate for at least 1 hour.

When the mushrooms have softened, use a slotted spoon to lift them from the liquid to a chopping block. Strain the soaking liquid through a double layer of cheesecloth to eliminate any grit or debris. Set the strained liquid aside. Using a chef's knife, roughly chop the mushrooms and reserve.

Heat the butter in a medium sauté pan over medium heat. Add the shallots and garlic and sauté for about 2 minutes, or just until softened. Add the wine, raise the heat, and bring to a boil. Lower the heat and simmer for about 4 minutes, or until reduced to 2 tablespoons.

Whisk in the flour, stirring to smooth. Whisking constantly, add the reserved mushroom soaking liquid. Add the peppercorns and allspice, along with salt to taste, and return to a boil. Lower the heat and simmer for about 15 minutes, or until reduced by almost half and thickened.

Strain the gravy through a fine-mesh sieve into a clean saucepan. Add the reserved porcini, along with the cream. Place over medium heat and bring to a simmer. Taste, season with pepper, and add more salt, if necessary. Simmer for 5 minutes.

Remove from the heat and stir in the herbs before serving.

# Turkey Roulade with Chestnut Stuffing

At the height of Delmonico's glory, turkey (or *dinde*, its French title) reigned almost supreme on the table. It was usually a small bird, about 8 to 10 pounds, and it was larded, boned, pieced, placed on intricate pastry or starch bases, and decorated beyond imagination. We have taken some of these ideas and translated them to a turkey roulade filled with a stuffing redolent with creamy, sweet chestnuts.

*6 tablespoons unsalted butter, at room temperature*

*1 small shallot, minced*

*5 tablespoons chopped flat-leaf parsley*

*2 tablespoons chopped fresh sage*

*1 boneless turkey breast half, skin-on and butterflied (see note)*

*Coarse salt and freshly ground pepper to taste*

*Chestnut Stuffing (recipe follows)*

*¼ cup canola oil*

*2 large carrots, peeled and cut into chunks*

*2 medium onions, peeled and cut into chunks*

*2 ribs celery, well washed, peeled, and cut into chunks*

*2 cups chicken broth*

*1 tablespoon cornstarch dissolved in 1 tablespoon cold water, if needed*

Place ½ cup of the butter in a shallow bowl. Add the shallot, ¼ cup of the parsley, and 1 tablespoon of the sage. Using a rubber spatula, work these aromatics into the butter. Set aside.

Place a piece of plastic film on a clean, flat work surface. Place the butterflied turkey breast on top of it and cover it with another piece of plastic film. Using a mallet or a small cast-iron frying pan, pound the breast meat out to make a rectangle about 12 by 8 inches. Lay the breast out with the long side facing you.

Using your fingertips, gently make little pockets under the turkey skin without tearing the skin entirely off the flesh, and force half of the herb butter into the pockets.

Melt the remaining herb butter in a small saucepan over low heat.

Using a pastry brush, lightly coat the interior flesh and the skin of the turkey with the melted herb butter. Season both sides with salt and pepper.

Press a ½-inch-thick layer of Chestnut Stuffing over the interior flesh, leaving a ½-inch border around the edges.

Begin making the roulade by rolling the long side up and over the stuffing. Continue rolling until you have formed a neat, tight roll, folding the ends in to compact the roll.

Using butcher's twine, carefully tie the roll in 2-inch intervals so that it will hold its shape as it cooks.

Preheat the oven to 350°F.

Heat the oil in a large sauté pan over medium-high heat. Add the turkey roll and sear, turning occasionally, for about 5 minutes, or until nicely colored on all sides. Using tongs, remove the turkey from the pan and set aside.

Place the carrots, onions, and celery in the bottom of a roasting pan to make an even bed for the roll. Place the roll on top of the vegetables. Add the chicken broth, place the pan in the preheated oven, and roast for about 40 minutes, or until an instant-read thermometer reads 155°F when inserted into the thickest part.

Transfer the roll to a serving platter. Tent lightly with aluminum foil and allow to rest for 15 minutes.

Transfer the vegetables and any remaining cooking liquid to the bowl of a food processor fitted with the metal blade or to a blender jar. Process to a smooth purée.

Place the purée in a saucepan and, if not thick enough, add the cornstarch mixture and bring to a simmer. Taste and, if necessary, season with salt and pepper. Cook for about 5 minutes, or until slightly thickened. Whisk in the remaining 2 tablespoons of butter. Fold in the remaining parsley and sage and remove from the heat.

Remove the butcher's twine from the roulade. Using a sharp knife, cut the roll crosswise into ½-inch-thick slices. Drizzle a bit of the vegetable gravy over the roll and serve with the remaining gravy passed on the side.

NOTE: If your butcher does not offer such a service, butterfly the turkey breast by simply laying the breast half on a clean work surface, skin side down, and, using a boning knife, remove the breast bone by slipping the knife between the bone and the flesh. Pushing slightly against the bone, follow the bone to its end. Using your fingertips, gently lift the breast bone out. Then, using a chef's knife, make an incision in the center of the breast and slice from the top to the end without cutting through the far side of the flesh. You should now be able to open the two breast pieces like a book.

## CHESTNUT STUFFING

*1 cup chopped dried figs*

*1-pound loaf brioche bread, cut into ½-inch cubes*

*2 tablespoons duck fat (see note) or unsalted butter*

*¾ cup chopped shallots*

*¾ cup chopped onions*

*½ cup chopped leeks*

*¼ cup chopped celery*

*12 ounces roasted chestnuts, chopped*

*¼ cup chopped flat-leaf parsley*

*1 tablespoon chopped fresh sage*

*1 large egg, beaten*

*Coarse salt and freshly ground pepper to taste*

*Up to 1 cup chicken broth, as needed*

Preheat the oven to 325°F.

Place the figs in a heatproof bowl. Add boiling water to cover by 2 inches and set aside to rehydrate for 1 hour. Drain well, discarding the soaking liquid, and set aside.

Bake the bread cubes on a nonstick baking tray, turning frequently, for about 15 minutes, or until golden brown and dry. Remove from the oven and set aside.

Heat the duck fat in a large, heavy saucepan over medium heat. Add the shallots, onions, leeks, and celery and sauté for about 5 minutes, or until the vegetables have softened but not taken on any color.

Some sample illustrations from *The Epicurean* showing ornate poultry presentation. Especially note the truffle-studded breast, below.

Remove from the heat and add the reserved figs, along with the chestnuts, stirring to combine well. Stir in the bread cubes, parsley, and sage. Add the egg and season with salt and pepper. The mixture should be soft and moist, not dry and stiff. If it seems too dry, add just enough chicken broth to moisten. Use as directed in the above recipe or transfer to a buttered baking dish and bake in a preheated 350°F oven for about 30 minutes, or until cooked through and nicely browned on top.

**NOTE:** Duck fat is available from D'Artagnan or other specialty butchers.

# French Breast of Pheasant with Butternut Squash Risotto

SERVES 6

Nothing says luxury like the phrase "pheasant under glass," although we have not been able to locate any recipe calling for this presentation. (We did find one that calls for the pheasant to be roasted and served on a large crouton decorated with its head and plumage.) We assume that the "under glass" came about because pheasant is so lean that it tends to dry out when cooked so it was covered with a glass dome to hold as much moisture as possible as it made its way from the kitchen to the dining room. Or perhaps it just looked terrific, particularly when adorned with its vibrant plumes.

We like to serve ours on a vividly orange risotto, but it is not necessary to do so to enjoy the lovely stuffed pheasant breast.

*6 pheasant breasts*

*Fruit Stuffing (recipe follows)*

*½ cup (1 stick) unsalted butter*

*Coarse salt and freshly ground pepper to taste*

*2 tablespoons corn oil*

*3 tablespoons minced shallots*

*¾ cup dry white wine*

*2 tablespoons apple cider vinegar*

*2 cups chicken stock*

*2 tablespoons chopped flat-leaf parsley*

*Butternut Squash Risotto, optional (see page 120)*

Using a small, sharp knife, clip each wing at the first joint, leaving the shoulder bone attached. Run the knife in a circle around the shoulder bone closest to the breast to loosen the meat. Then, using the knife, scrape the meat down and off the bone. Using a kitchen towel, clean the bone of any residual meat.

Still using the small, sharp knife, make an incision directly at the very top of the center of each breast. Slide the knife in almost to the bottom and from left to right to make a small pocket.

Place a heaping tablespoon of the stuffing into each pocket. Use a toothpick, inserted across the top, to fasten the pocket shut.

Preheat the oven to 375°F.

Melt 6 tablespoons of the butter and, using ¼ cup of it, generously coat the breasts. Season with salt and pepper.

Combine the remaining 2 tablespoons of melted butter with the oil in a large sauté pan over high heat. Add the pheasant breasts, skin sides down, and sear, shaking the pan from time to time, for about 7 minutes, or until the skin is golden and crisp. Transfer the breasts to a baking dish and roast for an additional 8 minutes, or until the meat is firm to the touch. Take care not to overcook or the meat will toughen. Remove from the oven and tent lightly to keep warm.

While the breasts are finishing, return the pan to medium heat. Add the shallots and cook for 1 minute. Stir in the wine and vinegar, bring to a boil, and cook for 2 minutes. Add the stock and remaining 2 tablespoons of butter and cook for about 8 minutes, or until reduced to a saucelike consistency. Stir in the parsley and season with salt and pepper.

If serving with the risotto, either pack the risotto into 3-inch round molds and then unmold it in the center of each of 6 large, shallow soup bowls or spoon

equal portions of the risotto into the center of each bowl. Place a pheasant breast on top and drizzle the sauce around the edge of the bowl. Alternatively, place a breast in the center of each of 6 dinner plates, drizzle the sauce over the top, and serve with whatever starch and vegetable suits you.

## FRUIT STUFFING

*1 tablespoon unsalted butter*

*2 tablespoons minced shallots*

*¼ cup finely diced Granny Smith apple*

*2 tablespoons brandy*

*2 tablespoons finely chopped dried apricots*

*2 tablespoons finely chopped dried plums (prunes)*

*1 tablespoon chopped toasted almonds*

*Pinch ground cinnamon*

*1 tablespoon fresh lemon juice*

*Coarse salt and freshly ground pepper to taste*

*1 tablespoon fresh bread crumbs*

Heat the butter in a medium sauté pan over medium heat. Add the shallots and sauté for about 2 minutes, or just until the shallots have begun to sweat their liquid. Add the apple and cook for another 3 minutes, or until the apples have softened. Add the brandy and cook for about a minute, or until the alcohol has burned off.

Stir in the apricots, plums, almonds, and cinnamon. When well blended, sprinkle on the lemon juice. Season with salt and pepper and remove from the heat.

Add the bread crumbs, stirring to blend. Set aside to cool before using.

# Squab with Foie Gras Braised Cabbage

SERVES 6

Squab, a young pigeon, has very rich but delicate dark flesh that calls for extraordinary measures when looking for an accompaniment. Often berries or deep red wines are used, but we decided to risk the farm and serve it with a luscious foie gras–flavored cabbage. This is truly a recipe that reflects the glory days of Delmonico's.

Although it is not necessary to serve the mustard sauce with this dish, it does add a note of elegance, as well as highlighting the mustard in the squab glaze. Since both it and the cabbage can be made in advance, we suggest that you make this lovely addition to the final dish.

*8 ounces Grade B foie gras (see page 87), trimmed of veins*

*Coarse salt and freshly ground pepper to taste*

*½ cup finely diced carrot*

*½ cup finely diced celery*

*½ cup finely diced fennel*

*½ cup finely diced leeks*

*½ medium red onion, peeled and cut into slivers*

*8 cups very thinly sliced Napa or Savoy cabbage or a mix combined with red cabbage*

*Approximately 2 cups chicken stock or fat-free broth*

*½ cup Italian truffle-flavored honey*

*1½ tablespoons Dijon mustard*

*6 boneless squab, halved*

*2 tablespoons canola oil*

*1 tablespoon unsalted butter*

*½ tablespoon chopped fresh sage*

*Mustard Sauce, optional (recipe follows)*

Heat a large, heavy saucepan such as a rondeau over high heat.

Season the foie gras with salt and pepper and place it into the hot pan. Sear, turning frequently, for about 3 minutes, or until nicely colored on all sides. Using tongs, remove the liver from the pan and place it in the freezer to firm up for 10 minutes. (If not using within 10 minutes, transfer to the refrigerator until ready to use.)

Lower the heat under the saucepan and add the carrots, celery, fennel, and leeks, stirring to coat them with the foie gras fat. Add the onion slivers and stir to combine. Add the cabbage and, using tongs, toss to coat it well with the fat. Add 1 cup of the stock and raise the heat. Bring to a simmer and season with

salt and pepper to taste. Lower the heat and cook, tossing frequently and adding more liquid as needed, for about 10 minutes or until the cabbage is just wilted.

Remove from the heat and transfer to a fine-mesh sieve to drain, reserving the cooking liquid if you plan to make the mustard sauce. (Don't bother washing the pan—you will be using it to finish the cabbage.)

Preheat the oven to 375°F.

Line a large baking pan with parchment paper that has been lightly coated with oil.

Combine the honey and mustard in a small mixing bowl. Set aside.

Season the squab with salt and pepper to taste.

Combine the canola oil and butter in a large frying pan over high heat. Add the squab, skin side down, in batches if necessary, and sear for about 4 minutes or until golden. Transfer the squab to the prepared baking dish, skin side up.

When all the squab halves have been seared, using a pastry brush, generously coat the skin with the honey-mustard mixture. Transfer them to the preheated oven and roast for 7 minutes or until cooked through.

While the squab is roasting, finish the cabbage.

Using a sharp knife, finely dice the chilled foie gras. Return the foie gras to the rondeau (used to cook the cabbage) and place over high heat. Season with salt and pepper and sear, stirring frequently, for about 3 minutes, or until the foie gras has rendered its fat and is crisp. Add the strained cabbage and toss to combine. Taste and, if necessary, add salt and pepper. Add the sage, tossing to combine.

Remove the squab from the oven.

Place equal portions of the cabbage in the center of each of 6 dinner plates. Place 2 squab halves over the cabbage, drizzle with Mustard Sauce, if using, and serve.

## Mustard Sauce

*1 tablespoon unsalted butter*

*2 cloves garlic, peeled and chopped*

*1 small onion, peeled and chopped*

*5 black peppercorns*

*1 bay leaf*

*2 cups dry red wine*

*2 cups beef stock or fat-free beef broth*

*1 cup reserved cabbage cooking liquid or chicken stock or fat-free chicken broth*

*1 tablespoon cornstarch, if needed*

*1 to 2 tablespoons Dijon mustard*

*Coarse salt and freshly ground pepper to taste*

*2 tablespoons heavy cream*

Heat the butter in a large saucepan over medium heat. Add the garlic and onion and sauté for 2 minutes. Stir in the peppercorns and bay leaf. When combined, raise the heat and add the wine. Bring to a boil. Lower the heat and simmer for about 20 minutes, or until the pan is almost dry. Add the beef and cabbage cooking liquid, raise the heat, and again bring to a boil. Lower the heat and simmer for 30 minutes or until reduced by half and thickened. (If the mixture does not have a saucelike consistency, dissolve 1 tablespoon cornstarch in 1 tablespoon cold water and whisk it into the sauce.)

Whisk in the mustard to taste and season with salt and pepper. When combined, whisk in the cream and remove from the heat.

Pour the sauce through a fine-mesh sieve into the top half of a double boiler set over very hot water and keep warm until ready to serve. Alternatively, transfer it to a covered container and refrigerate until ready to use. Reheat it, without allowing it to boil, when ready to serve.

# Duck Breasts with Pear Purée, Swiss Chard, and Dried Cherry Sauce

SERVES 6

Duck, duck, and more duck found its way to the elaborate tables of late-nineteenth-century America. Wild duck was abundant all along the Eastern seaboard, and hunting was a great sport among the rich. Presumably, restaurants obtained their catch from rugged men who spent their days in the wetlands. One of the most favored birds was the canvasback duck because it fed on wild celery, giving its flesh a highly aromatic flavor. Wild duck is still available through suppliers such as D'Artagnan (see Sources); however, for convenience we used the more readily available Long Island duck. Should time and money allow, do try this recipe using the wild.

Although the recipe has many components, much of the work can be done well in advance of serving. Some of the syrup from the Dried Cherry Sauce is used to marinate the duck, so it must be made in advance.

> *6 duck breasts*
>
> *¾ cup cherry sauce syrup from Dried Cherry Sauce (recipe follows)*
>
> *¼ cup light olive oil*
>
> *2 tablespoons champagne vinegar*
>
> *2 teaspoons freshly grated ginger*
>
> *½ teaspoon hot pepper sauce, or to taste*
>
> *1 star anise*
>
> *Coarse salt and freshly ground pepper to taste*
>
> *Pear Purée (recipe follows)*
>
> *Braised Swiss Chard (recipe follows)*
>
> *Dried Cherry Sauce (recipe follows)*
>
> *6 sprigs flat-leaf parsley, optional*

Using a small, sharp knife, trim excess fat from the duck breasts, leaving about ¼-inch layer.

Combine the cherry sauce syrup with the oil, vinegar, ginger, and hot pepper sauce in a resealable plastic bag. Add the duck breasts and star anise, seal, and refrigerate for 2 hours.

Cover the grill rack with aluminum foil and preheat on high.

Remove the duck breasts from the marinade and season with salt and pepper. Place the breasts, skin side down, on the aluminum foil. Cook for 4 minutes, then turn and cook for an additional 3 minutes.

Using tongs, remove the breasts from the grill. Pull off the aluminum foil and return the breasts to the hot grill rack. Grill, turning frequently to prevent burning, for another 2 minutes or until cooked to medium-rare (see note). Remove the breasts from the grill and set aside for 5 minutes.

Place 2 heaping tablespoons of the Pear Purée in the center of each of 6 dinner plates. Mound an equal portion of the chard at the top of each plate. Using a chef's knife, cut each breast on the bias into ½-inch thick slices, keeping each breast together. Fan a breast out across the bottom of each plate. Spoon some of the sauce over the duck and around the plate. If desired, garnish the top with a sprig of parsley, and serve.

NOTE: The USDA recommends cooking duck to an internal temperature of 165°F. We prefer to cook it a bit less than that, as the meat toughens once it gets past medium-rare.

## DRIED CHERRY SAUCE

*1 cup dried sweet cherries*

*1 cup port wine*

*½ cup balsamic vinegar*

*3 cups veal demi-glace (see note)*

*2 cups chicken stock or fat-free chicken broth*

*2 tablespoons unsalted butter, at room temperature*

*Coarse salt and freshly ground pepper, if needed, to taste*

Combine the cherries with the port and vinegar in a medium, nonreactive saucepan over medium-low heat. Bring to a simmer and cook gently for 12 minutes, or until the cherries absorb some of the liquid and the liquid itself becomes syrupy.

Remove from the heat and drain off the syrup. Measure out ¾ cup and reserve it for making the duck marinade. Return the remainder to the saucepan, along with the demi-glace and stock.

Return the saucepan to high heat. Bring to a boil, then lower the heat and simmer for about 20 minutes, or until reduced to a saucelike consistency. Taste and, if necessary, season with salt and white pepper.

Remove the sauce from the heat and keep it warm until ready to serve. Alternatively, transfer it to a covered container and refrigerate for up to 5 days. Reheat when ready to serve.

NOTE: Veal demi-glace is prepared with a rich, tomato-flavored brown sauce known as Espagnole sauce (one of the four "mother" sauces of classic French cuisine) that has been cooked with Madeira and additional rich, brown stock. It takes a great deal of preparation and cooking to make a great one. Fortunately, it is now available at specialty food stores or online (see Sources).

## PEAR PURÉE

*¼ cup (½ stick) unsalted butter*

*1 sprig rosemary*

*5 Bosc pears, peeled, cored, and quartered*

*1 cup dry white wine*

*1 tablespoon vanilla extract*

*½ cup sugar*

Place the butter in a small saucepan over low heat. Add the rosemary and heat just long enough to melt the butter. Remove from the heat, but keep warm and melted. Let stand for 30 minutes.

Combine the pears with the wine and vanilla in a medium heavy saucepan over medium heat. Add the sugar, stirring to combine. Bring to a simmer, then lower the heat and cook at a bare simmer for about 10 minutes, or until the pears are soft and the pan is almost dry. Remove from the heat.

Transfer the pear mixture to a blender jar or the bowl of a food processor fitted with the metal blade.

Remove the rosemary from the butter. Discard the rosemary. Add the flavored butter to the pears and process to a smooth light purée.

Keep the purée warm until ready to use. Alternatively, place it in a covered container and refrigerate for up to 3 days. Reheat before using.

## BRAISED SWISS CHARD

*½ cup olive oil*

*2 tablespoons chopped shallots*

*1 tablespoon chopped garlic*

*5 pounds red Swiss chard, well washed, trimmed of tough stems and chopped*

*1 cup fat-free chicken broth*

*Coarse salt and freshly ground pepper to taste*

*2 tablespoons unsalted butter, at room temperature*

Place the oil in a large, deep pan, such as a rondeau, over medium heat and add the shallots and garlic. Cook, stirring frequently, for about 3 minutes, or until fragrant. Add the chard, along with the broth and salt and pepper. Cover and cook, uncovering and tossing occasionally, for about 12 minutes, or until all the chard has wilted completely.

Remove the chard from the heat and add the butter, tossing to melt. Serve immediately or transfer to a container, cover, and refrigerate for up to 3 days. Reheat before serving.

Fish and shellfish were prominently featured on early Delmonico's menus. When multiple courses were presented, at least one fish dish was served, in addition to the oysters that often began the meal. Many dinners featured two or more fish dishes.

As with poultry, it was unheard of to present a simple grilled fish. Almost all the early recipes that we have encountered call for elaborate preparations and finish with a rich, cream-based sauce. Of course, some rules have not changed—the cook and diner alike were always encouraged to cook and eat fish and shellfish only when exceedingly fresh. However, frequently the diner was warned that the meat of most shellfish was easily digested only by "robust" stomachs!

Contemporary dining requirements have expanded the steak house menu to include many more fish and shellfish dishes than in the past. At Delmonico's we always offer a beautiful Lobster Newburg, as well as a few light fish dishes.

# Fish and Shellfish

DELMONICO'S LOBSTER NEWBURG

MOLDED SEAFOOD TURBAN WITH
CURRY CREAM SAUCE

YELLOWFIN TUNA WITH PICKLED VEGETABLES

ROASTED SALMON WITH ARTICHOKE
TOMATO VINAIGRETTE

FILET OF SOLE MARGUERY

SEARED SCALLOPS WITH SWEET CORN
PUDDING AND PINOT NOIR BEURRE ROUGE

Another Delmonico's fairy tale begins with a man named Ben Wenberg, a sea captain who sailed between Cuba and New York trading fruit. He was a thin man, a fancy dresser whose finery was custom made to fit his rail-like body. He was quite a gastronome and, when in New York, dined frequently at Delmonico's. He became a dear and trusted friend to Charles. At some point along about 1876, Wenberg announced that, in his travels, he had discovered a new way to cook lobster. He asked Charles Delmonico to bring a chafing dish and a lobster right to his table, where he proceeded to prepare the crustacean with cream, cognac, sherry, sweet butter, and cayenne pepper. Charles found it delicious and asked Chef Ranhofer to put it on the menu. Chef Ranhofer added his own refinements, and the dish was named "Lobster à la Wenberg" in its inventor's honor. As time passed, for an unknown reason, Captain Wenberg and Charles Delmonico had a disagreement and stopped speaking, so Charles removed the dish from the menu. However, it had become so popular that diners refused to let it go. Charles, ever the consummate host, quietly replaced the "wen" with "new" (and, perhaps, the "berg" with "burg"), and so the dish has remained. It was immortalized by Chef Ranhofer in *The Epicurean* as both "à la Newburg" and "à la Delmonico."

# Delmonico's Lobster Newburg

SERVES 4

Lobster Newburg is such a classic that there is not much you want to do to change it. Rich and delicious, we have added a bit of caviar to heighten its extravagance. It is not necessary to finish the dish, but it does add a touch of color and some salty brininess to mellow out the cream and brandy.

> *Two 1-pound live lobsters*
> *3 tablespoons unsalted butter*
> *½ cup diced carrot*
> *½ cup diced onion*
> *½ cup diced celery*
> *2 tablespoons tomato paste*
> *¼ cup plus 1 tablespoon brandy*
> *3 cups heavy cream*
> *Coarse salt and freshly ground white pepper to taste*
> *2 shallots, peeled and minced*
> *Cayenne pepper to taste*
> *Freshly ground nutmeg to taste*
> *1 large egg yolk, at room temperature*
> *1 tablespoon freshly squeezed, strained lemon juice*
> *1 ounce American sturgeon caviar, optional*
> *Brioche Batons (recipe follows), optional*

Place a lobster on a cutting board. Using a sharp chef's knife held vertically, plunge the point into the lobster's head about 1 inch behind the eyes. Push the knife completely in to touch the cutting board and then move it forward to cut the entire head in half. This is the quickest and easiest method of killing a live lobster. Pull the claws from the body. Prepare an ice water bath in a bowl large enough to hold all the lobster parts and set it aside.

Place the claws and bodies in the top half of a steamer over boiling water. Cover and steam the lobster for 4 minutes. Remove the bodies and continue steaming the claws for an additional 3 minutes. Immerse both the bodies and claws in the ice water bath as soon as you remove them from the steamer to stop the cooking.

Crack the shells on the bodies and claws and carefully remove the meat, keeping it in pieces as large as possible. Separately reserve the meat and the shells.

Preheat the oven to 350°F.

Place the lobster shells in a roasting pan in the preheated oven and roast, turning occasionally, for about 12 minutes, or until nicely colored and fragrant. Remove from the oven and set aside.

Heat 2 tablespoons of the butter in a large saucepan over medium heat. Add the carrot, onion, and celery and sauté for about 4 minutes, or just until the vegetables

begin to soften without taking on any color. Add the tomato paste and sauté for about 1 minute, or just until well-incorporated. Stir in the reserved lobster shells, followed by ¼ cup of the brandy. Cook for about 3 minutes, stirring to deglaze the pan. Add the cream, stir to blend, and raise the heat. Bring to a simmer and then immediately lower the heat to a gentle simmer. Season with salt and pepper and cook gently for about 1½ hours, or until very thick and well seasoned.

Remove the sauce from the heat and pour it through a fine-mesh sieve into a clean container, pressing on the solids to extract all the flavor. Discard the solids and set the sauce aside.

Heat the remaining tablespoon of butter in a medium sauté pan over medium-low heat. Add the shallots and season with cayenne and nutmeg. Cook, stirring constantly, for about 2 minutes, or until the seasonings have colored and are fragrant. Add the reserved lobster meat and sauté for 1 minute. Add the remaining tablespoon of brandy, stirring to deglaze the pan. Add the reserved cream sauce, raise the heat, and bring to a gentle simmer.

Place the egg yolk in a small bowl.

Remove from the heat and, using a slotted spoon, transfer an equal portion of the lobster meat to each of 4 shallow soup bowls. Whisk a bit of the hot sauce into the egg yolk to temper it and then whisk the egg mixture into the sauce. Add the lemon juice, taste, and, if necessary, adjust the seasoning with salt and pepper. Pour the sauce over the lobster in each bowl. If using, spoon an equal portion of the caviar into the center of each bowl and garnish with Brioche Batons. Serve immediately.

### BRIOCHE BATONS

> *1 loaf brioche bread*
> *½ cup (1 stick) melted unsalted butter*
> *Sea salt to taste*

Preheat the oven to 375°F.

Line a rimmed baking sheet with parchment paper. Set aside.

Using a serrated knife, slice the ends from the brioche. Then cut the brioche crosswise into ½-inch-thick slices. Trim the crust from all sides of each slice. Cut each slice into logs about ½ inch wide. You will need 5 pieces for each serving of the lobster. (If you have extra, make them anyway—they are terrific for breakfast or with cheese.)

Using a pastry brush, generously coat all sides of the brioche pieces with butter. Season with sea salt and place in a single layer on the prepared baking sheet.

Bake for about 7 minutes, or until golden and crisp. Remove from the oven and serve warm.

The toasts may be made in advance and reheated just before serving. Store, airtight, refrigerated for 3 days or frozen for 1 month. If frozen, reheating will take about 15 minutes.

**Lobster à la Newburg or Delmonico (*Homard à la Newburg ou à la Delmonico*)**

"Cook six lobsters each weighing about two pounds in boiling salted water for twenty-five minutes. Twelve pounds of live lobster when cooked yields from two to two and a half pounds of meat and three to four ounces of lobster coral. When cold detach the bodies from the tails and cut the latter into slices, put them into a sautoir, each piece lying flat, and add hot clarified butter: season with salt and fry lightly on both sides without coloring; moisten to their height with good raw cream; reduce quickly to half and then add two or three spoonfuls of Madeira wine; boil the liquid once more only, then remove and thicken with a thickening of egg-yolks and raw cream (No. 175). Cook without boiling, incorporating a little cayenne and butter; warm it up again without boiling, tossing the lobster lightly, then arrange the pieces in a vegetable dish and pour the sauce over."

As written in *The Epicurean* by Chef Charles Ranhofer

# Molded Seafood Turban with Curry Cream Sauce

SERVES 6

It is rare to see dishes such as this one on today's menus. Turbans (called such because of their shape) and timbales all now seem old-fashioned. However, this is so easy to put together and so reminiscent of early culinary elegance that it shines on a contemporary table.

Interestingly enough, we have found references to curry powder seasonings throughout the works of chefs Ranhofer and Filippini. It gives just a hint of heat and gentle color to this rich sauce.

*5 tablespoons unsalted butter, at room temperature*

*2 tablespoons fresh orange juice*

*2 tablespoons fresh lemon juice*

*2½ pounds boneless white fish filets, such as tilapia or flounder*

*Coarse salt and freshly ground white pepper to taste*

*1 pound shrimp, peeled, deveined, and chopped*

*2 large egg whites*

*1 cup heavy cream*

*2 tablespoons cognac*

*1 teaspoon minced fresh tarragon*

*1 teaspoon minced flat-leaf parsley*

*1 teaspoon minced fresh thyme leaves*

*Hot pepper sauce to taste*

*Curry Cream Sauce (recipe follows)*

*1 tablespoon minced chives*

*2 tablespoons caviar, for garnish, optional*

Preheat the oven to 350°F.

Using 3 tablespoons of the softened butter, generously butter a 5-cup ring mold. Set aside.

Combine the orange and lemon juices. Set aside.

Using a clean kitchen towel, pat the filets very, very dry. Sprinkle the juice mix over both sides of the filets, then season with salt and white pepper.

Line the mold with the filets, arranging them with the narrow ends to the center and leaving an overhang on both the inside and outside edges of the mold. If there are any dark spots on a filet, turn the dark side toward the interior.

Combine the shrimp with the egg whites, cream, cognac, tarragon, parsley, and thyme in the bowl of a food processor fitted with the metal blade. Process to a smooth purée. Season with hot pepper sauce and salt.

Scrape the shrimp purée into the filet-lined mold, patting firmly with a spatula to tamp the mixture down. Smooth the top and then fold the filet ends over the purée to completely cover.

Cut a piece of parchment paper to fit the top of the mold and melt the remaining 2 tablespoons butter. Using a pastry brush, generously coat it with butter. Brush the top of the mold with butter and cover it with the prepared parchment, buttered-side down.

Wrap the entire mold in aluminum foil. Place it in a large baking dish with enough hot water to come about 1 inch up the sides. Bake for about 30 minutes.

Remove from the oven and set the mold on a wire rack to rest for 5 minutes.

Remove the foil from the mold. Carefully remove the parchment paper and run a small, sharp knife around the edge to loosen the fish from the mold.

Place a serving platter over the mold and then invert to release the turban onto the platter. Spoon the Curry Cream Sauce over the top, sprinkle with chives and caviar, if using, and serve.

## CURRY CREAM SAUCE

*¼ cup (½ stick) unsalted butter*

*¼ cup Wondra flour (see page 75)*

*1 tablespoon curry powder*

*¼ teaspoon freshly grated orange zest*

*Coarse salt and freshly ground white pepper to taste*

*1 cup heavy cream, warm*

*2 large egg yolks, at room temperature, beaten*

*¼ cup sherry*

*1 tablespoon fresh lemon juice, strained*

Melt the butter in the top half of a double boiler over boiling water. Whisk in the flour and curry powder. When well blended, whisk in the orange zest and season with salt and white pepper. Beat in the cream and cook, stirring constantly, for about 5 minutes or until thickened.

Place the egg yolks in a small mixing bowl. Whisking constantly, beat about ¼ cup of the hot cream mixture into the yolks. When well blended, add the tempered egg yolks to the hot cream mixture in the top of the double boiler, beating constantly. Whisk in the sherry and continue to cook, stirring constantly, for about 5 minutes, or until the sauce is very hot and thick.

Remove from the heat and strain through a fine-mesh sieve into a clean container. Whisk in the lemon juice. Taste, season with salt and pepper if necessary, and serve immediately. If not serving immediately, wash and dry the top half of the double boiler and return the sauce to it. Place it over hot water to keep warm until ready to use.

# Yellowfin Tuna with Pickled Vegetables

SERVES 6

This is another recipe on the current Delmonico's menu that acknowledges contemporary diners' interest in Asian flavors. It is also one of our most frequently requested dishes (beyond the Delmonico steak). Although it has a number of components, they can all be made in advance; only the tuna needs to be cooked at the last minute.

> *Six 6-ounce center-cut tuna loins about 3½ by 2½ inches each*
> *Coarse salt to taste*
> *¾ cup cracked mixed peppercorns (pink, black, and white)*
> *¼ cup peanut oil*
> *Pineapple Chutney (recipe follows)*
> *Pickled Vegetables (recipe follows)*
> *Truffled Pineapple Soy Sauce (recipe follows)*

Generously season the tuna with salt, then roll 3 sides into the cracked peppercorns, leaving the bottom and ends uncoated.

Heat the oil in a large sauté pan over medium-high heat. Add the tuna, pepper-coated side down, and sear for 1 minute, pressing down slightly on the tuna just until the color begins to change. Sear the remaining pepper-coated sides for 1 minute each. Finally sear the uncoated side for 30 seconds. The tuna should now be medium-rare.

Transfer the tuna pieces to a clean cutting board. Using a serrated knife, cut each piece crosswise, into six pieces.

Fan one tuna loin out in the center of each dinner plate. Make a quenelle (see page 155) of chutney at one side and place a mound of Pickled Vegetables on the other. Drizzle the plate with the Truffled Pineapple Soy Sauce and serve.

## PINEAPPLE CHUTNEY

*1 cup sugar*

*2 kaffir lime leaves*

*1-inch-long piece ginger, peeled*

*1 stalk lemon grass, trimmed and cut into 1-inch pieces*

*1½ cups chopped fresh pineapple*

Combine the sugar with 1 cup water in a small, heavy saucepan over high heat. Bring to a boil, then lower the heat and simmer for 5 minutes.

Add the lime leaves, ginger, and lemon grass and simmer for another 5 minutes. Stir in the pineapple and bring to a boil.

Remove from the heat and set aside for 2 hours.

Remove the lime leaves, ginger, and lemon grass and serve.

The chutney may be stored in a covered container and refrigerated for up to 1 week.

## PICKLED VEGETABLES

*¼ cup peanut oil*

*3 tablespoons rice wine vinegar*

*Juice and zest of 1 lime*

*Juice and zest of 1 lemon*

*2 tablespoons light soy sauce*

*1 teaspoon hot pepper sauce*

*2 tablespoons sugar*

*1 teaspoon minced garlic*

*1 medium carrot, peeled, cut into a fine julienne, and blanched*

*1 medium leek, white part only, well washed, cut into a fine julienne, and blanched*

*1 medium hothouse cucumber, trimmed and cut into a fine julienne*

Combine the oil and vinegar in a medium mixing bowl, whisking to blend well. Add the lime and lemon juices and zests and whisk to combine. Whisk in the soy sauce and hot pepper sauce. When blended, stir in the sugar and garlic.

Combine the carrot, leek, and cucumber in a large mixing bowl. Add the pickling mix and, using your fingertips, toss to coat well.

Cover and refrigerate at least 2 hours or overnight before serving.

## TRUFFLED PINEAPPLE SOY SAUCE

*¼ cup heavy cream*

*1 cup sugar*

*¾ cup light soy sauce*

*¾ cup bottled clam juice*

*¾ cup fat-free chicken broth*

*½ cup pineapple juice*

*1 tablespoon cornstarch dissolved in 3 tablespoons cold water*

*1½ tablespoons truffle oil (see page 119)*

*Coarse salt and freshly ground pepper, if necessary*

Place the cream in a small, heavy saucepan over medium heat. Bring to a simmer and cook, watching carefully to prevent boil-over, for about 5 minutes, or until reduced to 2 tablespoons. Remove from the heat and set aside.

Combine the sugar with ½ cup water in a medium heavy saucepan over low heat. Bring to a simmer and cook for about 10 minutes, or until the sugar begins to turn light brown and the liquid is reduced to 1 cup.

Add the soy sauce, clam juice, chicken broth, and pineapple juice, raise the heat, and bring to a boil. Reduce the heat and simmer for about 25 minutes, or until reduced by half. Beat in the cornstarch mixture. Return to a boil and, whisking constantly, boil for 1 minute. Add the reserved reduced cream, along with the truffle oil, and return to a simmer.

Remove the sauce from the heat and set it aside to cool. Taste and, if necessary, adjust the seasoning with salt and pepper. Serve at room temperature.

# Roasted Salmon with Artichoke Tomato Vinaigrette

SERVES 6

Salmon is, without a doubt, one of the most popular fish today. With its health benefits, availability, and delicate flavor, it has truly become the chicken of the sea. This is a very simple recipe—you don't really even need the vinaigrette, as the marinade creates a flavorful fish that can stand on its own.

*¾ cup light olive oil*

*4 sprigs rosemary*

*3 cloves garlic, peeled and chopped*

*1 large onion, peeled and chopped*

*2 tablespoons fresh thyme leaves*

*Six 7-ounce boneless, skinless salmon filets*

*Coarse salt and freshly ground pepper to taste*

*2 tablespoons canola oil*

*Artichoke Tomato Vinaigrette (recipe follows)*

Combine the oil with the rosemary, garlic, onion, and thyme in an extra-large resealable plastic bag. Add the salmon, seal, and toss to coat the fish. Refrigerate for 1 hour or up to 8 hours.

When ready to cook, preheat the oven to 375°F. Alternatively, oil a grill and preheat it to high.

Remove the fish from the bag and, using your fingertips, clean off any small pieces of the marinating vegetables or herbs. Season both sides with salt and pepper.

Heat the oil in a large ovenproof sauté pan over medium-high heat. When it is very hot but not smoking, add the salmon, skin side up. Sear for 4 minutes, or until evenly browned on the flesh side. Turn the fish and sear the skin side for 2 minutes. Transfer the pan to the preheated oven and roast for about 5 minutes, or until the salmon is still almost rare in the center (unless, of course, you prefer your fish well done). Alternatively, grill the salmon for about 5 minutes per side on the hot grill.

Place a salmon filet on the center of each dinner plate. Spoon some of the vinaigrette over the top and serve.

"The salmon is a large fish, its weight reaching thirty pounds. The body is covered with scales, the meat is tender, thick, red colored and delicate, of an exquisite taste, but very difficult to digest." So said Charles Ranhofer.

## ARTICHOKE TOMATO VINAIGRETTE

*2 tablespoons olive oil*

*2 shallots, peeled and chopped*

*1 clove garlic, peeled and chopped*

*¼ cup dry white wine*

*Juice and zest of 2 lemons*

*½ cup bottled clam juice*

*2 tablespoons white wine vinegar*

*Coarse salt and freshly ground pepper to taste*

*2 tablespoons unsalted butter, at room temperature*

*½ cup finely diced tomatoes*

*½ cup finely diced canned artichoke hearts*

*½ cup finely sliced green or black olives*

*1 tablespoon chopped flat-leaf parsley or chives*

Heat the oil in a medium saucepan over low heat. Add the shallots and garlic and sauté for 2 minutes, or until softened. Add the wine, raise the heat, bring to a boil, and cook for 3 minutes, or until reduced by half. Add the lemon juice and zest, clam juice, and vinegar and simmer for 3 minutes. Season with salt and pepper and remove from the heat. Set aside until cool.

Strain the cooled mixture through a fine-mesh sieve into a clean saucepan, discarding the solids.

Place the saucepan over medium heat and bring to a simmer. Lower the heat and, whisking constantly, beat in the butter. When the mixture is well emulsified, remove it from the heat and fold in the tomatoes, artichokes, and olives. Taste and, if necessary, adjust the seasoning with salt and pepper. Fold in the parsley or chives and serve warm.

# Filet of Sole Marguery

SERVES 6

This classic French dish was served throughout the years of Delmonico's enormous influence on American dining. It is simple to put together, delicious, and if you like, it can be prepared in individual gratin dishes for presentation directly at the table. We don't add the lobster butter required by many nineteenth-century chefs, but if you have it on hand, certainly use it!

*½ cup plus 3 tablespoons unsalted butter, at room temperature*

*1½ pounds filet of sole or other delicate white fish filets*

*2 cups fish stock (or a combination of equal parts bottled clam broth and fat-free chicken broth)*

*¾ pound shrimp, peeled and deveined*

*1 cup (about 18) shucked oysters, well-drained*

*¼ cup Champagne*

*4 large egg yolks, beaten, at room temperature*

*Coarse salt and freshly ground white pepper to taste*

*1 tablespoon chopped chervil (see note)*

Preheat the oven to 325°F.

Using 3 tablespoons of the butter, generously coat the interior of a large, shallow baking dish.

Arrange the fish filets in a single layer over the bottom of the dish. Pour 1 cup of the fish stock over the top. Place the shrimp and oysters over the fish. Cover the dish with aluminum foil without allowing the foil to touch the fish.

Bake for 15 minutes, or just until the fish is cooked through.

While the fish is cooking, place the remaining 1 cup fish stock in the top half of a double boiler directly over high heat. Bring to a boil and boil until reduced by half.

Place the top half of the double boiler into the bottom half over boiling water. Whisk in the Champagne and when hot, add the remaining ½ cup of butter, whisking until emulsified.

Place the egg yolks in a small mixing bowl. Whisking constantly, beat about ¼ cup of the hot Champagne mixture into the yolks. When well blended, add the tempered egg yolks to the hot mixture in the top of the double boiler, beating constantly. Season with salt and white pepper and continue to cook, still whisking, for about 5 minutes, or until the sauce is smooth and thick.

Remove the fish from the oven and turn the oven temperature to broil.

Uncover the fish and carefully transfer it to a heatproof serving platter. Pour the sauce over the top and place the platter under the broiler. Broil for 3 minutes, or until bubbling and golden brown.

Sprinkle the filets with chopped chervil and serve.

NOTE: Chervil is a very delicate and often expensive herb, but its flavor is unique and marries so well with the richness of this dish that we suggest you use it if possible. If not, parsley will work just fine.

*The Epicurean* (Recipe No. 1273): Soles à la Marguery-Fillets (*Filets de Sole à la Marguery*) "Raise the fillets from two clean, skinned soles; fold in two, pare nicely and season, range them on a buttered baking dish and bestrew the surface with shallots and mushroom peelings: moisten to cover with a white wine court bouillon and allow the liquid to come to a boil, then finish cooking the fillets in a slow oven. Drain them off singly, and dress on a dish; garnish one side with shrimp tails, and the other with blanched oysters, from which the hard parts have been removed, or mussels. Keep the whole very warm. Strain the broth the soles were cooked in, reduce it to half-glaze, thicken with a mere spoonful of Normande sauce and finish with a piece of fresh lobster butter; pour this over the fillets and garnishings, then glaze the sauce with a gas salamander; two minutes will suffice for this. When the fish is ready to be served, brush the surface with thin lines of red butter."

# Seared Scallops with Sweet Corn Pudding and Pinot Noir Beurre Rouge

SERVES 6

In looking at early recipes for scallops, we found that the preparations were about the simplest of any we had seen. They stayed within the realm of classic French marinière, au gratin, orly, and St. Jacques à la Parisienne preparations. This recipe blends a bit of Americana and a bit of France, combining the sweet corn pudding and the classic beurre rouge.

> *2 tablespoons unsalted butter, plus more if needed*
>
> *2 tablespoons peanut oil, plus more if needed*
>
> *¼ cup finely diced sweet onion*
>
> *1 cup finely sliced shiitake mushrooms*
>
> *3 cups fresh corn kernels (or frozen, thawed and drained of excess water)*
>
> *Coarse salt and freshly ground pepper to taste*
>
> *18 diver's scallops (about 2 pounds, see note)*
>
> *2 tablespoons julienned scallions*
>
> *6 Sweet Corn Puddings (recipe follows)*
>
> *Pinot Noir Beurre Rouge (recipe follows)*
>
> *Fresh herb sprigs for garnish*

Preheat the oven to low.

Heat 1 tablespoon each of the butter and oil in a large nonstick sauté pan over medium-high heat. Add the onions and sauté for 1 minute. Stir in the mushrooms and cook, stirring and tossing, for about 4 minutes, or until the mushrooms have wilted. Add the corn, season with salt and pepper, and continue to cook, stirring and tossing, for about 4 minutes or just until the corn has softened and begun to release its milk.

Scrape the mixture onto a plate, tent lightly with aluminum foil, and keep warm in the oven. Using a paper towel, wipe the pan clean.

Season the scallops with salt and pepper to taste.

Return the sauté pan to medium-high heat and add the remaining 1 tablespoon each of butter and oil. When very hot but not smoking, add the scallops and sear for 2 minutes or until golden on one side. Turn and sear for 2 more minutes, or until the other side is golden. If necessary, do this in batches using clean butter and oil each time.

Transfer the scallops to a nonstick baking sheet and keep them warm in the oven while you begin the plates.

Toss the scallions into the corn mixture and spoon about ½ cup of the mixture into the center of each of 6 dinner plates. Unmold a corn pudding on top of each plate. Place 3 scallops in a triangle shape around the pudding. Drizzle the plates with the beurre rouge, garnish the puddings with a sprig of fresh herb, and serve.

NOTE: Also known as "day-boat" scallops, diver's scallops are caught in the wild and delivered to market within a day. They often have the roe attached. If you can't get these super-fresh bivalves, it is important that those you do purchase be extremely fresh and dry-packed, that is, without being treated with a preservative.

## SWEET CORN PUDDING

*1 cup heavy cream*

*1½ cups fresh corn kernels (or frozen, thawed and drained of excess water)*

*1 tablespoon chopped leek, white part only*

*3 tablespoons unsalted butter*

*2 large eggs*

*1 tablespoon truffle oil (see page 119)*

*Coarse salt and freshly ground pepper to taste*

Place ½ cup of the cream in a medium heavy saucepan over medium heat. Add 1 cup of the corn and leeks and bring to a simmer. Lower the heat and cook at a gentle simmer for about 10 minutes, or until the corn is very tender.

Preheat the oven to 350°F.

Generously butter the interior of six 4-ounce ramekins. Set aside.

Remove the corn mixture from the heat and pour it into a blender jar. Cover and, holding the lid down with a kitchen towel to prevent the heat from pushing it upward, process to purée.

Combine the eggs with the remaining ½ cup of cream in a medium mixing bowl. Add the truffle oil, beating to incorporate. Slowly whisk in the corn mixture. Season with salt and pepper.

Carefully pour the corn mixture into each prepared ramekin, filling it about three quarters full. Place the filled ramekins into a large baking dish, and add just enough cool water to fill the baking dish about halfway. Cover the entire dish with aluminum foil.

Bake for about 35 minutes, or until the tip of a small, sharp knife inserted into the center of the pudding comes out clean.

Serve the puddings hot. If you are not ready to serve yet, transfer the ramekins to a wire rack to cool. Cover with aluminum foil for a maximum of two hours and, before serving, reheat in a 350°F oven for 10 minutes or until very hot.

## PINOT NOIR BEURRE ROUGE

*2 cups Pinot Noir or other spicy, rich red wine*

*3 small shallots, peeled and sliced*

*1 bay leaf*

*¼ cup sugar*

*¼ cup chopped ginger*

*1 tablespoon black peppercorns*

*1 cup heavy cream*

*½ cup (1 stick) chilled unsalted butter, cut into pieces*

*Coarse salt and freshly ground pepper to taste*

Place the wine in a medium heavy saucepan. Add the shallots, bay leaf, sugar, ginger, and peppercorns. Place over medium heat and bring to a boil. Lower the heat and simmer for about 12 minutes, or until reduced to ½ cup liquid.

Add the cream, stirring to blend well. Return the mixture to a boil. Immediately lower the heat to a bare simmer and cook for about 10 minutes, or until reduced to ¾ cup. Begin whisking in the butter, a bit at a time, beating to emulsify. When all the butter has been incorporated, season with salt and pepper and remove from the heat.

Strain the mixture through a fine-mesh sieve into the top half of a double boiler, discarding the solids. Place the pan over very hot (but not boiling) water. Keep warm until ready to serve.

It would impossible for the pastry kitchen in any modern restaurant to replicate the dessert presentations of Delmonico's golden age. Almost without exception, desserts were extraordinary molded extravaganzas featuring spun and pulled sugars, candied fruits, woven pastry, small cakes, ice creams, and all manner of mind-boggling ornamentation. These *pièces montées* were always followed with bonbons, petits fours, glazed and candied fruits, and other small sweets.

Molded ice cream dishes and bombes were particular favorites. One of the most interesting recipes we found was for asparagus ice cream that was prepared in two parts—one pale green and the other dark green to imitate the asparagus tip. The two colors were molded into the shape of a bunch of asparagus spears and served tied with spun sugar ribbon. Another recipe was for a tomato-shaped mold to be lined with strawberry ice, filled with burnt almond ice cream in which a mixture of macerated fruits and macaroons was centered,

# Desserts

RASPBERRY NAPOLEONS

BAKED ALASKA

ROASTED FIGS WITH SCENTED SABAYON
AND PISTACHIOS

CRÊPES SUZETTE

WARM FINANCIERS WITH
MILK CHOCOLATE BRITTLE SAUCE

BRIOCHE BREAD PUDDING
WITH RUM RAISIN SAUCE

MIXED FRUIT WITH CHICORY SALAD
AND BLEU D'AUVERGNE

Spun sugar, pastry, and other sweets create an elaborate nineteenth century dessert centerpiece.

When the Delmonico brothers opened their little café and pastry shop on Williams Street in 1827, along with cigars and rich, flavorful coffee; dark, foamy hot chocolate; and a soupçon of brandy, the brothers offered an array of fine cakes prepared by Peter. Costing but a penny a serving, among the cakes sitting in the window were Bavarois, Gâteau Breton, Tarte Franchonette, and Savarin. Up until the latter part of the twentieth century, many of these cakes were still served by the slice in restaurants all over the world. Only in recent years have individual desserts been served in a restaurant setting.

and served with a vanilla ice cream–based sauce flavored with *prunelle* (wild plum liqueur).

A famous series of feasts, known as the Silver, Gold, and Diamond dinners, was commissioned by three of New York City's most distinguished gentlemen, Leonard Jerome (the future father-in-law of Sir Winston Churchill), banker August Belmont, and lawyer and man-about-town William R. Travers. In the course of executing these dinners, the pastry kitchen at Delmonico's created some acclaimed desserts. Among them was an innovative *pièce de résistance* prepared for the Jerome dinner—truffled ice cream, a dessert that would be right at home in the inventive contemporary restaurant.

Because we now feature such an array of steak-and-potato dishes and because contemporary diners have many more dietary considerations, for the most part our dessert menu features simple confections. However, we like to think that even in their simplicity, our desserts still offer a sweet ending to a sumptuous meal.

# Raspberry Napoleons

SERVES 6

The napoleon is in the classic French tradition, although it may not be a French dessert at all. Some historians link it to a Danish pastry chef who lived in the early part of the nineteenth century, but it seems that by the Victorian era, napoleons, or *mille-feuilles* (translates as "thousand leaves" for the flaky pastry layers) as they were called, were popular in France and around the world.

This simplified version uses frozen strudel dough in place of the traditional puff pastry. You could, of course, replace the strudel dough with frozen puff pastry, baking it according to the package directions.

*½ teaspoon unflavored gelatin*

*2 cups half and half*

*½ cup sugar*

*1 vanilla bean*

*3 large egg yolks*

*1 large egg*

*Pinch salt*

*¼ cup Wondra flour (see page 75)*

*1 cup plus 2 tablespoons unsalted butter, chilled*

*1 package frozen strudel dough, thawed according to manufacturer's directions*

*1 cup superfine sugar*

*3 cups fresh raspberries, plus more for garnish*

*3 tablespoons confectioners' sugar*

*Grand Marnier Raspberry Sauce (recipe follows)*

*6 sprigs mint*

Combine the gelatin with ¼ cup cold water in a small saucepan. Allow the gelatin to bloom for 1 minute. Then, place the saucepan over low heat and cook, stirring constantly, for about 1 minute, or until the gelatin has melted. Remove from the heat and set aside.

Combine the half and half with ¼ cup of the sugar in a heavy saucepan. Using a small, sharp knife, split the vanilla bean in half lengthwise, scrape the seeds into the half and half, and add the split bean. Place the mixture over medium heat and bring to a boil. Immediately turn off the heat, but leave the pan on the burner to keep warm.

Combine the egg yolks with the whole egg and salt in a medium mixing bowl. Add the remaining ¼ cup sugar, whisking to incorporate.

Sift the flour over the egg mixture, whisking to combine.

Working quickly, whisk about half of the hot half and half into the egg mixture. Whisking constantly, pour the tempered egg mixture into the hot half and half in a slow, steady stream. Place over medium heat and cook, still whisking constantly, for about 3 minutes, or until the mixture is thick. Add the reserved gelatin, whisking well to incorporate. Continue to cook and stir the mixture for another 2 minutes. Whisk in 2 tablespoons of the chilled butter. When well blended, remove the pastry cream from the heat and pour it into a clean container.

Place a piece of plastic film over the top of the pastry cream, smoothing it out to cover the surface completely. Cover and refrigerate for about 4 hours, or until well chilled.

Cut a 2-by-4-inch piece of heavy cardboard to use as a pattern. Set aside.

Line 2 baking sheets with parchment paper. Preheat the oven to 375°F. Melt the remaining 1 cup butter and set aside.

Peel off one layer of the thawed strudel dough, covering the remaining dough with a slightly damp clean kitchen towel to keep it from drying out.

Carefully lay the piece of strudel dough out on a clean, flat work surface.

Using a pastry brush, lightly coat the entire surface with melted butter. Then, sift a very fine layer of superfine sugar over the top. Continue layering, buttering, and sugaring the dough until you have three 4-layer stacks of dough.

Using the cardboard pattern, cut 21 rectangles of layered strudel dough. (You will only need 18, but this will give you a couple of extras to allow for breakage.)

Place the dough rectangles on the prepared baking sheets, taking care not to crowd the pan. Once each pan is filled, lay a piece of parchment paper over the dough and then place another baking sheet on top to hold the dough flat.

Place the pans in the preheated oven and bake for about 5 minutes, or until the dough is golden, crisp, and slightly caramelized. Watch carefully, as the dough can go from golden to overcooked very quickly.

Remove from the oven and set aside to cool.

Using an offset spatula, carefully transfer the cooled rectangles from the parchment to wire racks. Go slowly—the dough is very fragile.

Remove the pastry cream from the refrigerator and stir to smooth out.

Place 6 rectangles on a clean, flat work surface. Carefully spoon an equal portion of the cream over each. Nestle a few raspberries into the cream and then spoon another thin layer of cream over the raspberries. Top with another dough rectangle and then make another layer of pastry cream, raspberries, and pastry cream. Place the final dough rectangle on top. Sift confectioners' sugar over all.

Spoon equal portions of the Grand Marnier Raspberry Sauce into each of 6 dessert plates. Carefully place a napoleon in the center. Garnish each plate with a few raspberries and a sprig of mint. Serve immediately.

### GRAND MARNIER RASPBERRY SAUCE

*2½ cups fresh raspberries*

*2 tablespoons fresh orange juice*

*2 tablespoons Grand Marnier or other orange-flavored liqueur*

*3 tablespoons sugar*

*1 teaspoon freshly grated orange zest*

Combine all the ingredients in a medium saucepan over medium heat. Cook, stirring occasionally, for about 5 minutes, or until the raspberries are soft. Remove from the heat.

Transfer the mixture to the bowl of a food processor fitted with the metal blade. Process to purée.

Scrape the purée into a fine-mesh sieve and, pushing with a rubber spatula, press to extract all the purée, leaving any seeds and zest behind.

Pour the sauce into a clean container. If not using immediately, cover and refrigerate for up to 3 days.

# Baked Alaska

SERVES 6

Although Baked Alaska was not invented at Delmonico's, it was given its familiar name in the 1860s by Charles Ranhofer, in honor of the purchase of the Alaska territory by the United States. Up to this time, it had been known by its classical French name, *omelette Norvégienne.* At one point, Ranhofer called it the Baked Florida-Alaska and featured banana ice cream in the center. Over the years, there have been many versions of this dessert, all of them having an ice cream core surrounded by some type of pastry, which is then covered with whipped cream or meringue and given a quick bake or broil to brown the exterior while leaving the interior frozen.

At Delmonico's, Baked Alaska is one of the most frequently requested desserts. The ice cream and cake flavors change to reflect the seasons. Although we serve it in individual portions at the restaurant, this recipe is for one large cake meant to be cut into individual slices. Just know that it makes a fabulous statement, however it is presented!

*1½ quarts caramel or dulce de leche ice cream,*
*or other ice cream of choice (see note), softened slightly*

*Devil's Food Cake Layer (recipe follows)*

*2¼ cups sugar*

*10 large egg whites, at room temperature*

*½ teaspoon cream of tartar*

*¼ teaspoon salt*

Line a 9-inch, 1½-quart stainless-steel mixing bowl with plastic film, leaving about a 3-inch overhang around the edge.

Using a rubber spatula, transfer the ice cream to the bowl, smoothing the top with the spatula. The entire bowl should be filled. Place in the freezer for about 3 hours or until completely solid.

Place the cake on a small baking sheet. Remove the ice cream from the freezer and invert the bowl onto it. Grabbing the plastic film that lines the bowl, lift the bowl from the ice cream and discard the plastic film. Again, return the dessert to the freezer and chill for about 1 hour, or until the cake is hard.

Preheat the oven to 400°F.

Combine the sugar and 1 cup water in a medium saucepan over medium-high heat. Attach a candy thermometer to the side of the pan and cook, stirring occasionally, for about 12 minutes, or until the mixture reaches the soft-ball stage, or 240°F on the thermometer.

Remove from the heat and keep warm.

Place the egg whites in the bowl of a standing electric mixer fitted with the wire whip and beat on medium-high until very foamy. Add the cream of tartar and salt, increase the speed to high, and beat until soft peaks form. Immediately begin pouring the hot syrup into the whites, allowing it to drizzle down the sides of the bowl to keep from splattering. Continue to beat on high until the mixture is cool and very shiny. (This is known as an Italian meringue.)

Remove the molded ice cream cake from the freezer, leaving it on the baking sheet. Using a rubber spatula, immediately begin spreading the meringue over the frozen ice cream, covering the entire dessert in a thick, even layer, shaping the meringue into soft peaks over all.

Once the dessert is covered, immediately bake it for about 8 minutes, or until the meringue is lightly browned and the ice cream is soft enough to be pierced with a metal cake tester or skewer.

Remove the Baked Alaska from the oven and carefully transfer it to a serving plate. Cut into slices as for a standard cake and serve.

NOTE: Häagen-Dazs, available in most supermarkets, makes an excellent dulce de leche ice cream.

## DEVIL'S FOOD CAKE LAYER

*6 tablespoons Dutch-processed cocoa powder*

*¾ cup sugar*

*½ cup plus 2 tablespoons hot milk*

*1 cup sifted cake flour*

*½ plus ⅛ teaspoon baking soda*

*½ teaspoon salt*

*½ cup vegetable shortening*

*1 large egg*

*1 teaspoon vanilla extract*

Lightly grease the bottom of a 9-inch round cake pan. Cover with a piece of parchment paper (or wax paper) cut to fit exactly. Lightly grease the paper and set the pan aside.

Preheat the oven to 350°F.

Place the cocoa in a small, heatproof bowl. Add 2 tablespoons of the sugar, mixing to blend. Gradually whisk in the milk, beating until blended. Set aside to cool.

Combine the flour, baking soda, and salt with the remaining sugar. Sift into a stainless-steel mixing bowl. Add the shortening, along with half of the cooled cocoa mixture, beating on low with a handheld electric mixer. Add the egg and vanilla along with the remaining cocoa mixture. Raise the speed to medium and beat to blend, scraping down the sides of the bowl with a rubber spatula from time to time.

Scrape the batter into the prepared cake pan, gently smoothing the top with a spatula. Bake for about 25 minutes, or until a cake tester inserted into the center comes out clean.

Remove the cake from the oven and place it on a wire rack to cool for 5 minutes. Then invert the pan onto the wire cake rack and tap it to release the cake from the pan. Peel off the paper and allow the cake to cool completely.

Either use the cooled cake immediately or wrap it in plastic film and refrigerate for up to 2 days or freeze until ready to use as directed in the recipe. This cake may also, of course, be iced and served as a simple cake.

# Roasted Figs with Scented Sabayon and Pistachios

SERVES 6

A dessert with inviting aromatic scents, this is easy to make and presents beautifully. It is just rich enough to say "dessert," but light enough to not be indulgent.

The figs can be roasted early in the day and reheated just before serving, and the sabayon can be made a day or two in advance and heated by setting it in a bowl of very warm water when ready to use.

*½ cup lavender honey*

*½ teaspoon ground cardamom*

*18 fresh figs, well washed and dried*

*4 large egg yolks*

*¼ cup superfine sugar*

*⅛ teaspoon ground coriander*

*½ cup Riesling*

*⅓ cup chopped, toasted pistachios*

Preheat the oven to 400°F.

Line a baking sheet with parchment paper. Set aside.

Combine the honey and ¼ teaspoon of the cardamom in a small saucepan over low heat, stirring to combine. When hot, remove from the heat.

Using a pastry brush, lightly coat the figs with the spiced honey. Place the coated figs on the prepared baking sheet about ½ inch apart and roast them for about 5 minutes, or until nicely glazed and heated through.

Remove the figs from the oven and tent lightly to keep warm.

Heat water to just simmering in the bottom half of a double boiler. Keep it hot while you begin the sabayon.

Combine the egg yolks with the sugar, coriander, and remaining ¼ teaspoon of cardamom in the top half of a double boiler directly over low heat. Cook, whisking constantly, for about 12 minutes, or until the mixture is very thick and pale yellow. You don't want to heat it too quickly, however, or it will curdle. Whisk in the wine and then scrape down the sides of the pan with a rubber spatula.

Immediately set the pan into the bottom half of the double boiler over the simmering water. Cook, scraping down the sides of the pan and stirring constantly with the spatula, for about 7 minutes, or until the mixture is very thick but light, and mounds slightly when lifted with the spatula.

Spoon an equal portion of the sabayon into the center of each of 6 dessert plates. Using the back of a spoon, gently spread the sauce out over the plates to completely cover the bottom. Place 3 figs in the center of each plate, sprinkle with pistachios, and serve immediately.

# Crêpes Suzette

SERVES 6

Crêpes Suzette was all the rage on late-nineteenth-century menus. It is said that it was invented in 1895 by Henri Charpentier when, as a young chef in Monte Carlo, he had inadvertently ignited the crêpe sauce he was preparing tableside for the Prince of Wales. The resulting dessert caused such a sensation that the prince requested it be named after one of the female guests, Princess Suzanne. Although Charpentier recounted the event in his book, *Life à la Henri—Being the Memories of Henri Charpentier*, there is some dispute about its veracity. Apparently these delicious crêpes were on menus in Paris prior to 1895. They certainly made their way to turn-of-the-century American menus around the same time. Henri Charpentier did come to America, where, among other jobs, he served as private chef to John Rockefeller.

You will need both a 7 ½-inch crêpe pan and a chafing dish to properly prepare this dessert.

¼ cup (½ stick) unsalted butter

½ cup fresh orange juice, strained

1 teaspoon fresh lemon juice

6 tablespoons sugar

2 tablespoons Triple Sec

2 tablespoons cognac

Sweet Crêpes (recipe follows)

½ cup Grand Marnier or other orange-flavored liqueur

18 pieces candied orange peel

6 sprigs mint

Heat the butter in a large sauté pan over medium heat. Add the orange and lemon juices. Stir in the sugar and, stirring constantly, bring to a simmer. Cook for about 3 minutes, or until the mixture has thickened slightly. Add the Triple Sec and cognac and simmer for another minute.

Place one of the crêpes into the sauce. As it absorbs a bit of the liquid, carefully fold it in half and then fold the half into a triangle shape. Continue this process until all the crêpes are in the sauce.

Take the entire pan to the table. Pour the Grand Marnier over the crêpes and, holding the pan away from your face and your guests and using a fireplace match, carefully ignite the liqueur. Let the flames die out.

Using tongs, carefully place 2 crêpes on each of 6 dessert plates. Spoon sauce over the top and garnish with a bit of candied orange peel and a sprig of mint.

## Sweet Crêpes

*½ cup all-purpose flour, sifted*

*4 teaspoons sugar*

*Pinch salt*

*3 large eggs*

*¾ cup milk*

*1 tablespoon cognac*

*3 tablespoons melted unsalted butter*

*¼ cup clarified butter*

Combine the flour, sugar, and salt in a mixing bowl.

Combine the eggs, milk, cognac, and melted butter in a blender jar, processing to blend. Add the flour mixture and process to make a thin batter.

Pour the batter into a clean container, cover, and refrigerate for up to 30 minutes or as long as 2 days.

When ready to make crêpes, return the batter to room temperature. Transfer it to a pitcher or measuring cup with a pour spout. Set aside.

Cut twelve 8-inch square pieces of waxed paper or plastic film. Place one piece on a plate and set the plate and the remaining pieces of paper or film alongside.

Heat a nonstick crêpe pan over medium heat. Using a paper towel, lightly coat it with clarified butter.

Stir the batter and then pour about 2 tablespoons into the hot pan. Immediately lift the pan off the heat and swirl and rotate it to evenly coat the bottom with a thin layer of batter. Return the pan to the heat and cook for about 45 seconds or until the top is set and the bottom is golden brown.

Using your fingers to pry an edge loose, carefully lift and turn the crêpe to cook the remaining side. Cook for about 1 minute, or until lightly browned.

Place the first crêpe on the paper- or film-lined plate. Cover with another piece of paper or film. Continue buttering the pan and making and stacking crêpes until you have 12.

If the crêpes are not used immediately, they can be kept stacked, separated by waxed paper or plastic film, wrapped tightly, in the refrigerator for up to 1 day or the freezer for up to 1 month.

*Dining at Delmonico's*

# Warm Financiers with Milk Chocolate Brittle Sauce

SERVES 6

This archetypal French confection is often served with a simple sabayon sauce (see page 205), but we like to give it a contemporary garnish to accent the aroma of almond that swirls up from the warm cake. The financiers can be made early in the day and warmed just before serving, and the sauce can be made up to 2 weeks in advance.

*1 cup (2 sticks) plus 2 tablespoons unsalted butter*

*2¾ cups confectioners' sugar*

*½ cup plus 1 tablespoon all-purpose flour*

*½ cup plus 1 tablespoon blanched almond flour (see note)*

*7 large egg whites, at room temperature*

*1 teaspoon freshly grated lemon zest*

*Milk Chocolate Brittle Sauce (recipe follows)*

*6 small wedges almond brittle for garnish*

Preheat the oven to 300°F.

Using 2 tablespoons of the butter, generously coat the interior of six 4-inch round molds. Set aside.

Place the remaining 1 cup of butter in a small saucepan over low heat until melted, then cook for about 5 minutes, or until brown and very fragrant. Remove from the heat but keep warm.

Combine 2½ cups of the confectioners' sugar with the all-purpose and almond flours. When combined, sift twice to lighten.

Place the sifted dry ingredients into the bowl of a standing electric mixture fitted with the wire whip. Add the egg whites and beat, on low, until very well blended. Scrape down the sides of the bowl with a rubber spatula. With the motor running on low, slowly add the warm butter. Raise the speed to medium and beat until well-combined. Add the lemon zest and beat to blend.

Divide the batter among the prepared molds and bake for about 20 minutes, or until the cakes are firm to the touch, the tops are golden brown, and a cake tester inserted into the center comes out clean.

Transfer them to wire racks to cool for 15 minutes.

Invert the molds onto the wire racks and tap the cakes free. Place about ¼ cup of confectioners' sugar in a fine-mesh sieve and lightly dust the cakes.

Spoon some chocolate sauce onto each of 6 dessert plates. Place a financier in the center. Stick a small wedge of almond brittle into each cake and serve.

NOTE: Blanched almond flour is available from most specialty food stores or online (see Sources).

## MILK CHOCOLATE BRITTLE SAUCE

*½ cup chopped milk chocolate*

*½ cup chopped semisweet chocolate*

*1 teaspoon vanilla extract*

*⅔ cup milk*

*2 tablespoons heavy cream*

*2 tablespoons unsalted butter, at room temperature*

*½ cup chopped nut brittle, preferably almond*

Combine the chocolates in a small heatproof bowl. Add the vanilla and set aside.

Combine the milk and cream in a small saucepan over medium heat. Bring to just a simmer and cook gently for 1 minute. Immediately remove from the heat and stir in the butter.

Pour the hot milk over the chocolate. Let stand for about 1 minute, then beat vigorously to melt the chocolate. When smooth, add the nut brittle.

If not using the sauce immediately, do not add the brittle. Transfer the sauce to a clean container, cover, and refrigerate. When ready to use, reheat it over very low heat. Remove from the heat and stir in the nut brittle.

# Brioche Bread Pudding with Rum Raisin Sauce

SERVES 6 TO 8

Bread and rice puddings were favorite desserts throughout the nineteenth century and into the twentieth, both in dining rooms and at home. After a lull in their popularity, home-style desserts again became *de rigeur* in the early twenty-first century. This particular bread pudding is rich with buttery brioche, cream, and rum. Although we have made it in one big dish, if you prepare individual puddings, you will have an elegant dinner party dessert with old-fashioned flavor.

> *3 tablespoons unsalted butter*
>
> *1½-pound loaf brioche bread, cut into cubes*
>
> *1 cup golden raisins*
>
> *2½ cups cream*
>
> *3 large eggs*
>
> *¾ cup sugar*
>
> *¼ cup rum*
>
> *2 teaspoons vanilla extract*
>
> *1 teaspoon ground cinnamon*
>
> *Rum Raisin Sauce (recipe follows)*
>
> *Glazed Walnuts (recipe follows)*

Generously coat the interior of an 8-inch round or square baking dish with all the butter.

Place the bread cubes in a mixing bowl and add the raisins, tossing to blend well. Pack the bread mixture into the prepared baking dish.

Combine the cream with the eggs in a medium mixing bowl, whisking to blend well. Add the sugar, rum, vanilla, and cinnamon, whisking vigorously until the sugar has dissolved.

Pour the cream mixture over the bread, patting it down slightly to ensure that the bread soaks up the liquid. Cover the entire pan with plastic film and let rest for 1 hour.

Preheat the oven to 350°F.

Unwrap the pudding and bake it for about 1 hour, or until the top is golden and puffy and the edges have slightly pulled away from the pan.

Remove the pudding from the oven and let stand for 10 minutes before cutting.

When ready to serve, place a square of pudding in the center of each of 6 or 8 dessert plates. Spoon warm Rum Raisin Sauce over the top and garnish with the walnuts.

## RUM RAISIN SAUCE

*¾ cup sugar*

*1½ teaspoons cornstarch*

*½ cup golden raisins*

*¼ cup dark rum*

*1 tablespoon unsalted butter, at room temperature*

*½ teaspoon freshly grated lemon zest*

Sift the sugar and cornstarch together into a mixing bowl. Set aside.

Combine the raisins with 1 cup boiling water and bring to a boil over medium heat. Lower the heat and simmer for 15 minutes. Whisk in the reserved sugar mixture, whisking until well blended. Simmer for an additional 15 minutes, or until the sauce is quite thick.

Remove the pan from the heat and beat in the rum, butter, and lemon zest. If not using immediately, transfer to a covered container and store, refrigerated, for up to 1 week. Reheat before serving.

## GLAZED WALNUTS

*¾ cup light brown sugar*

*¼ cup honey*

*½ pound shelled walnuts*

*1 teaspoon vanilla extract*

Line a baking sheet with parchment paper. Set aside.

Combine the sugar and honey with ¼ cup water in a medium heavy saucepan over medium heat. Bring to a boil and cook without stirring for about 15 minutes, or until a candy thermometer inserted in the center reads 242°F.

Remove the syrup from the heat and stir in the nuts and vanilla. Let cool slightly and then stir again until creamy.

Transfer the nuts to the parchment-lined baking sheet and separate them with a table fork. Let stand until dry.

Store, in layers and tightly covered, for up to 2 weeks.

# Mixed Fruit with Chicory Salad and Bleu d'Auvergne

SERVES 6

Is this a dessert or a salad or a cheese course? We like to think that it is a little of all three, and most satisfying at the end of a rich meal. All the elements combine to make a slightly sweet yet tart finish. Each type of fruit could be made in larger amounts and served, alone, along with crème fraîche, mascarpone cheese, or even ice cream as a refreshing dessert.

*½ cup chopped dried apricots*

*½ cup dried cranberries*

*½ cup chopped toasted almonds*

*2 small heads chicory, well washed, dried, and pulled into small pieces*

*Zinfandel Vinaigrette (recipe follows)*

*Poached Pears (recipe follows)*

*Roasted Peaches and Quinces (recipe follows)*

*12 ounces Bleu d'Auvergne or other creamy blue cheese*

Combine the apricots, cranberries, and almonds. Set aside.

Place the chicory in a medium mixing bowl. Add just enough of the vinaigrette to lightly coat, tossing to blend well.

Place an equal portion of the dressed chicory in the center of each of 6 luncheon plates. Place 1 pear fan at the top of the plate and then 2 pieces each of the quince and peach at equidistant points so that the fruits form a triangle around the chicory. Sprinkle the dried fruit and nut mix over the chicory. Slice the cheese into 6 wedges and place one on each plate. Drizzle the plate with the reserved pear poaching syrup and serve immediately with warm, sliced cranberry-nut, pecan-raisin, or other dense nutty bread on the side.

## ZINFANDEL VINAIGRETTE

*1 cup Zinfandel wine*

*1 tablespoon sugar*

*1 sprig thyme*

*3 tablespoons red wine vinegar*

*1 tablespoon Dijon mustard*

*¾ cup peanut oil*

*Coarse salt and freshly ground pepper to taste*

Combine the wine with the sugar and thyme in a small nonreactive saucepan over medium-high heat. Bring to a boil, then lower the heat and simmer for about 10 minutes, or until reduced to ¼ cup. Set aside to cool.

Transfer the cooled wine mixture to a small mixing bowl. Remove and discard the thyme. Add the vinegar and mustard and, whisking constantly, beat in the oil. Season with salt and pepper and continue to whisk until well emulsified. Set aside until ready to use. You may have to whisk to re-emulsify the dressing before using.

## POACHED PEARS

*2 cups Zinfandel wine*

*1 cup sugar*

*1 cinnamon stick*

*½ vanilla bean*

*1 lemon, halved*

*3 Forelle pears, peeled*

Combine the wine with the sugar and cinnamon stick in a medium nonreactive heavy saucepan. Using a small, sharp knife, split the vanilla bean lengthwise and scrape the seeds into the wine. Then add the split bean. Squeeze the lemon juice into the saucepan and add the squeezed lemon halves. Place over medium heat and bring to a boil.

Lower the heat and simmer for 10 minutes. Add the pears, raise the heat, and bring to a boil. Lower the heat, cover, and simmer, turning the pears occasionally, for 25 minutes, or until the pears are tender and evenly cooked through.

Set the pan aside to cool.

Using tongs, carefully remove the cooled pears from the liquid. Set them aside.

Strain the liquid through a fine-mesh sieve into a small saucepan and bring it to a boil over medium-high heat. Lower the heat and simmer for about 15 minutes, or until reduced to a syrupy consistency. Remove from the heat and reserve for use as a sauce for the pears.

Using a chef's knife, cut the poached pears in half. Core and cut each half into quarters to yield 8 equal wedges.

Using a small, sharp knife, carefully cut each wedge into 2 or 3 thin slices without cutting through the bottom so that you can fan each wedge out. Reserve for use in the above recipe.

### Roasted Peaches and Quinces

> *2 large quinces, peeled, halved, and cored*
>
> *2 large peaches, peeled, halved, and pits removed*
>
> *½ cup Sauternes*
>
> *¼ cup pure maple syrup*
>
> *2 tablespoons melted unsalted butter*
>
> *½ teaspoon ground cinnamon*
>
> *¼ teaspoon freshly grated nutmeg*

Preheat the oven to 350°F.

Using a sharp knife, carefully cut the quinces lengthwise into 1-inch-thick slices. Place in a mixing bowl. Add the peach halves, along with the wine, syrup, butter, cinnamon, and nutmeg, tossing to coat well.

Place the coated fruit on a nonstick baking pan and bake, turning occasionally. Watch carefully—the peaches will bake in about 15 minutes, while the quinces will require about 25 minutes to be tender.

Remove from the oven and set aside to cool.

# Sources

## Meat and Game

D'Artagnan
800-327-8246
www.dartagnan.com

Hudson Valley Foie Gras
845-292-2500
www.hudsonvalleyfoiegras.com

Niman Ranch
866-808-0340
www.nimanranch.com

Jamison Farm Lamb
800-237-5262
www.jamisonfarm.com

## Fish and Shellfish

Browne Trading Company
800-944-7848
www.brownetrading.com

Wild Edibles
212-687-4255
www.wildedibles.com

## Fruits and Vegetables

Frieda's
800-241-1771
www.friedas.com

Chef's Garden
800-289-4644
www.chefs-garden.com

## Truffles and Caviar

Petrossian
800-828-9241
www.petrossian.com

Urbani Truffles and Caviar
www.urbanitruffles.com/about.asp

## Cheese

Artisanal Premium Cheese
877-797-1200
www.artisanalcheese.com

Murray's Cheese Shop
888-692-4339 x7
www.murrayscheese.com

# Index